the love connection

the **love** connection
WHY WE ARE HERE

THE LOVE COLLECTION

Library and Archives Canada Cataloguing in Publication

Christine, 1963-
The love connection : why we are here / Christine & Creator.

ISBN 978-0-9865978-0-0

1. Love. 2. God--Love. 3. Spirituality.
I. Creator (Spirit) II. Title.

BF575.L8C557 2010   152.4'1   C2010-902632-2

2010 © The Time of Love Unlimited
Printed in Canada.
Published by The Time of Love Unlimited.
This book was co-created by Christine and Creator.
www.thetimeoflove.com

welcome

Co-creation is the process of connecting to our Creator and doing something, anything, everything together! It is always loving and always facilitates the growth of all involved. We are blessed when we co-create, for this is the relationship that all of us are capable of being part of and it is what we were created for! We are all truly co-creating whenever we act in love!

This book is a work of love. It is a work of love for all of us and this "us" includes our Creator. Our Creator is only love. Love encompasses all in existence and draws all in, surpassing barriers, limitations and labels. It transcends all division. Because of this, our Creator has not been identified by gender-specifc terms such as "he" or "she". These words limit all that our Creator is. In these writings, we have had to use the word "it" because there is no word in the English language that articulates this encompassing concept.

This book is a work of love. It is intended to remind us of things we know and to help us to see, with loving eyes, how we are a miraculous creation of love and how we are already embodying this! It is intended to empower and inspire all of us to connect and to begin our own co-creative relationship, as we were all created to do. It is intended to give us all a "foundation" with which to continue becoming what we were truly created to be.

This book is the first in a series of material comprising The Love Collection. These writings have arisen out of an on-going process of healing and connecting more and more deeply to "self" and to the Source who created us all.

We are all one. Created out of love...

table of contents

the only question   1

beautiful beginnings   3

love experiencing   13

love perpetuating... love, in perpetuity   29

the truth of being created from love   41

the many gifts of love   49

thoughts of love   59

all you need is...   75

love, eternal   91

of love, love and more love   105

the intelligence of love   115

love. now is the time.   123

addendum

nutrition for the unified (non-dualistic) brain   127

the only question

All of creation is one perfect being, created out of love. It began with the loving thought of our Creator and our Creator's desire to have something to love. Out of that thought and out of that desire, we arose.

We were created out of love, to love and to be loved. This is the profound and absolute truth of existence.

It is this truth that we must remember and base all action upon. It is this truth that is changing and has changed the world in which we live. It is this truth that is the catalyst for the new time upon the earth that is now emerging. It is this truth that is the very catalyst of our entire evolution.

Love is what we are made of and love is what we were created to do and to be. But how do we do this? How do we be what we were created to be? How do we live this truth?

And how do we merge into the new time upon this earth that all of us are meant to be part of?

To answer these questions, we must begin by answering: What is love?

beautiful beginnings

Where we must start in understanding love and therefore in understanding what we are, is right at the very beginning! We must begin by eradicating untruths that stand in the way of connecting to all that we truly are and connecting to all that created us.

We are love. We were not created in "sin" or in pain or in shame. We were created in love and love is what we are doing at every moment of our existence.

It is just that sometimes our bodies don't remember or understand this.

Most of the ways in which we think about our existence do not focus on the cosmic, eternal nature of the stuff of which we are made. This concept must be brought into all understandings about what we are and how we are meant to live our lives in order for them to have any meaning and any truth. We were created in a moment, in a flash, in a bang by our Creator, whose sole motivation for doing so is to love us. It is that simple and it is that clear. What we have been doing since that creative moment, slightly more than 13.7 billion years ago, is evolving into absolute love in every aspect of our being as a whole creation.

Because we were created to be an experiential form of love; that is, a form of love that is capable of being interactive in loving and being loved, we have been evolving an experiential form to do so in. That is why physicality has come into being at all. However, the physicality of creation, created to embody and experience love, has had to evolve or grow until it became advanced enough to be what it truly was created to be.

Our entire evolution has been a long and beautiful love story. And we have been an active part of it.

Because we were created out of the energy of Creator who is only love, this love had to "divide" itself in order to have something to create us out of. This something is our essence and, in truth, it means that we are one with our Creator, equal to it and meant to be so. It is just that we have been in a period in our physical evolution where we have been too "immature" to be fully equal because we have been growing the physical form we are to occupy. While we are in our essence form (soul) we are fully engaged in co-creating our magnificent physical evolution into love.

This division from what created us is what is known as the first condition of existence. In order to come into being, we had to be "divided" out of what made us because that is all that existed to make us out of. It is this division, or rather it is our perception of it, that makes us feel separated from all that we truly are and all that made us while we are in our physical form.

We say it is our perception of this division that makes us feel separated because, in truth, there is no separation. It is only when we are in our bodies that we are unable to see past the perceived division and know the full meaning of all that we are. When we are in our soul form, we understand that there is truly no separation and we understand what our evolution since the first moment of creation has been about. To say that we have been co-creating ourselves since the moment we were created is absolute truth.

We have been co-creating ourselves because this is a two way relationship. It is a relationship based on interacting in "to love and to be loved". Therefore, as we have come into being, becoming defined and becoming who we are, so has our Creator become defined and who it is. We are all love, coming into an embodiment of love expressed, and we are all becoming the many forms of love expressed. This is mutual. It is interactive. It is intertwined. It is encompassing.

For it is love and love is all of these things.

Love has no beginning and love has no end. It simply is. It is the only true thing in existence. It is this absolute truth that we must use to break down the barriers that appear to separate us from the truth of what we are and what made us, and that therefore separate us from being all that we are when we are in our physical forms.

of love and "laws"

So let's go back to the first creative moment again.

In the beginning, there was only love. This love was – and is – Creator.

Where did this love come from?

It just *was*. Cosmically and eternally, it just *was* and *is*.

This love desired to have something to love and to be loved by and so this love "divided" itself and created something to love. It had to "divide" itself because itself was all that there was in existence.

When love divided loveself, it was pure energy. This energy needed to become a form that was experiential; that is, it needed to become a form that could take the action of loving and being loved. It needed to be more than just the energy of thought because, previously it had only been the energy of thought and that did not enable it to be *active* in loving. Thus it was that the love that created us began to put in place several laws or concepts that would enable the energetic thought and desire of love to become something to love and to be loved by.

In other words, these laws came into place to create our very physicality and our interaction with what created us.

Because half of the energy of love had come into being a "separate" thing at one time, it is right to say that creation began all at once. However, as the laws came into being so that the creative energy could become an experiential form, they created the phenomenon known as evolution. It would be correct to say that the laws are the tools of a certain period of our existence known as our evolution to date. In and of themselves, they create many conditions that we perceive as reality. It is this reality that forms the present physical world.

It is this reality that we are beginning to transcend or grow out of, for we are becoming what we have been created to be, fully, now.

When love "divided" itself to create something to love and to be loved by, this was the first law. We will call this first law duality. Because the only thing in existence was love, this first law created the illusion that there are things that are not love (or dualistic to it). It is this law that created the illusion of separation.

The second law was time. Time gave the evolution an order – it meant that some things would come into physical form before others and it meant that all would evolve.

The third law that was created was the law of motion. This law was also necessary to allow the separation or movement between Creator and Created. Coupled with duality, even though in truth we are one, this movement makes us also able to interact as two beings; therefore we are able to experience love in relation to one another in all ways.

The fourth law was space. To put it simply, it is this law that has allowed things within creation to expand even as they have contracted. One example of its effects is the fact that the universe (creation) has gotten bigger even as it has condensed to form more complex life within it.

The fifth law was gravity. Again, to keep things simple, we will define gravity as a force that draws things together.

The sixth law was polarity. In this sense of the word, we mean that something follows a specific course in relation to what else is happening around it.

The seventh law was the law of the dimensions. This law came into being because things that were not in physical form needed a place to be in existence, as did the things that were in physical form. Our world and the physical universe around it is referred to as the physical dimension.

These are the laws of creation or the laws of existence put in place by Creator for the sole purpose of creating something to love and to be loved by. And this something to love and to be loved by is us. It is all of creation. In other words, it is all of the energy of the big bang, now come into being in a physical formation. It is life.

It is made of absolute pure love and it is infused by the absolute pure intelligence that love is.

This is what we are. This, in our purest and most absolute state, is what we are and have been created to be.

So why does the world not reflect that?

It is because the seven laws govern physical matter and cause it to evolve until it can contain all the love it was made of, that the world does not reflect our pure and absolute state yet. The seven laws have been needed to cause us to evolve our physical matter and only our physical matter until we can be a physical embodiment of what our souls are, of love in action, of love experiencing, of love interacting with our Creator whom is only love.

emerging into love

Ever since we have been created, we have known that we were only working toward a time when we could become what we were created to be. Ever since we have been created, we have worked hand in hand with our Creator to further that growth. Together we have worked toward this cosmic goal with dedication, strength, faith and all of the other gifts of love. Together we have fostered and guided our physical matter until it can be all of the love that we truly are, in our most absolute and pure essence.

We need to look past the limits of the physical world, seeing past the illusions of separation created by the seven laws, and understand what we truly are and what it truly is that made us. This understanding is what we must focus on to become what we have been created to be. This understanding is what we must focus on in order to access the divine intelligence – love – that we are and that made us. In truth, our physical bodies are presently the smallest part of what we are! This does not mean that they are of less value than the rest of us; rather, it means that the activity they carry out is meant to represent so much more.

It is time to move past the limits created by the seven laws and become our cosmic eternal selves, our absolute true loving selves. These laws are temporary tools anyway, used only to bring us through a certain part of our creative evolution. Their purpose is now served.

For on December 30, 2006, all of the creation became ready to fully be what it was created to be. At this time, the physical matter that all of creation is had evolved to the point where it can now contain all of its' pure and absolute essence. At this time, the seven laws began to merge back into their original state and all that is not love began to cease to exist.

Over the next several years, we will continue to see this. We will continue to move out of the period whereby we have been evolving within the framework of the seven laws and we will see our true and absolute state emerging throughout creation. We will be what we have been created to be and we will create the world we were meant to live in. We will be one with what created us and it will all be about love and only love. Together with our Creator, we will co-create this phase of our evolution also, just as we have every other. We will do this by becoming all that we truly are and all that we truly are, is love.

love experiencing

All of this takes us back to the question posed in the introduction to this book: What is love? For us to be what we are, we have to understand what we are fully. And for us to understand what we are fully, we have to be what we are. Both are true. It takes both to make things complete. We are idea and matter for we are energy, made manifest. We are the love of our Creator, made into physical form.

Because we were created as an experiential form of love, it is often simplest for us to know love by what it does and this is where we will begin. The Source of All thought of love as a concept and then created us to experience love with and to be love with. Therefore, our definitions of love have to include what it does in order for us to understand it.

Love is tangible. Love is creative. Love is truth. Love is what Creator and Creation is and does.

Many strange ideas about love have crept into our belief systems over the course of our long evolution. This is purely due to duality and the other laws that helped us evolve our physical matter out of the energy of love. By eliminating these ideas we will gain a clearer understanding of love, for we will use the tool of knowing what it is by what it is not.

At the same time we will also see how applying love in actuality, to all aspects of our life, helps us to understand more fully what it is. We will become aware of how very much we do this and how very much in tune with love we truly are. In this writing, we will examine situations where love can be applied when it hasn't and see how it changes the outcome for all of creation. In this way, we will see how easy it is to know and to be love.

the one-ness of love

First of all it is necessary to say that love is an energy that encompasses. It is duality that caused the perception of division or separation. Love never sees anything as separate. It does not perceive of division. In other words, love does not exclude anything or anyone. It does not value one thing over another because, in truth, all are equal in this vast and beautiful thing known as creation. All in creation are one, created at one moment, out of one thing. It is only due to the laws that governed the evolution of this one-ness into physical form that some things are perceived as "older" and some "younger", some "first" and some "last", some "simple and some "complex" and so on within the whole one thing that creation is.

Our one-ness, our connection to one another and to our Creator, is the primary state that exemplifies the encompassing energy of love. In truth, there is no such thing as separation, even as we are individuals. A common thought that comes from duality is that we have to be one great big thing *or* an individual. But love is so encompassing, it includes both concepts as truth at the same time! We are one *and* we are individuals. We are individuals within the one that we all are. This concept alone gives us much to consider in how we enact within our individual lives, for nothing we do is done in isolation and everything we do affects the wholeness that we are part of.

This is easy to forget if one has forgotten the basic truth that we are more than the immediate bodies we occupy. If one stays focused on the truth that all in creation is cosmic and eternal, coming in and out of physical forms as we evolve those physical forms until they can contain all that is cosmic and eternal about us, it becomes much more clear.

By focusing on the eternal aspect of all that we are and all that we have been evolving toward, we can understand the whole point of taking loving action, even in a world caught up in unloving (dualistic) actions. When we realize that, while they sometimes may not be having apparent influence at the moment we make them, our loving actions always have the effect of helping creation evolve cosmically in the long term, it gives them much worth indeed.

Love is eternal. It is cosmic. It never dies and it never leaves. It only grows and grows until it encompasses more and more and more.

Love encompasses all in creation without beginning or end.

Love is the true energy that existed before creation began, after all, and everything is made of it. When we truly make decisions from love, these decisions encompass all that they affect, instead of choosing one thing or one person over another. Love does not exclude. This is the true state of love.

The truth that sometimes gets forgotten in the decisions people make is that this encompassment or inclusiveness is not limited just to people themselves! Under the illusion of being separate, decisions are often made in favor of people's interests that are not good for other people, other species and even for the earth itself.

A simple and obvious example to use is that of pesticides and herbicides. In an attempt to alter the environment to look like what a group of people have decided it should look like, much harm and death occurs. The interesting thing is that in evoking harm and death to other species and to the land through the application of these substances, we are now seeing how deeply and completely they affect the species that invented them! It took a while to see and to understand the harm and there are still those in resistance to the obvious truth that harm is occurring. However, the effects of these products are now causing a multitude of health problems for human beings as well.

The fact is, when decisions are made that have the potential to harm something in the whole body of creation, these decisions eventually come back to harm those who made them. It is only because we are all one and the decisions are not based on love that they can have this effect.

Love encompasses all in creation without beginning or end.

Love, applied truly, would have found a solution that did not cause harm or death to any living thing (and all things are living). A loving solution that fostered and fed the existing naturally producing ecosystem, thereby contributing to its health, would have been enacted instead with only positive results for all things within it.

That is love! Love causes all to thrive and to flourish! It does not question anything else's right to exist, for it understands that because something exists, it is a necessary and beloved part of the creation. Everything in creation is made out of the primary element that is love; it is only the law of duality and the other laws that have given it an intent or appearance of being other than love.

In fairness to humankind, it is the most complex part of the creation and it has been evolving in duality for almost 4.7 million years. Therefore, decisions that can divide and value one thing as desirable over another are only part of its evolution to this point. And, of course, this duality is not limited to human beings! Animal species and plant species and so on, kill one another for territorial and other "reasons" that have arisen as part of the period of evolution within the seven laws. But these "reasons" only exist within the limits of physical matter and the whole point of the physical matter itself is so that it can grow to encompass all that we truly are.

Therefore, the only way we have been able to move forward out of the limits of our physical experience is to aspire to attain the kind of elevated understanding that our Creator and our own soul essence contain. This cannot be done by staying focused merely on the world around us and its dualistic activities. We have to move into connection with what we truly are and what created us in order to evolve in a true sense. We have to focus on love and on its cosmic and eternal meanings.

This begins with awareness that we are something more than this dualistic world.

our true need

Love encompasses all in creation without beginning or end. When we know that all in creation is love, created by love, we can comprehend the absolute truth that all that exists is necessary and valued. Therefore, we no longer have to assign value to things. The value is there because they exist. We have only to accept that they are part of creation and love them and include them lovingly in what we do.

Several limiting belief systems can be shed once we comprehend the truth that love is encompassing and inclusive of everything in creation. A major one we can be rid of is the belief that we have to sacrifice things in order to show love and in order to receive it. Love never asks that we sacrifice or give up or do without anything. What this means is that true love includes everyone and everything in the solution or action taken, including you!

The concept that it is "good" to do without and to sacrifice certainly does not arise from an understanding of what love truly is. What's more, this kind of concept feeds another great and limiting untruth: that of there being not enough in creation for everything within it. These two untruths often go hand in hand and have had great "power" to alter lives in very negative ways. In other words, these two belief systems have been tools in the hands of the interests of those who serve things that are not loving, such as greed, control and so on.

This leads us to another absolute truth about love: love meets all needs.

It must be stated that the primary need of everything in existence is the very thing it was created for! That is, the primary need of everything in existence is to love and to be loved.

Love meets all needs. And the true need of each living thing is to love and to be loved. Therefore, our true needs get met every time we are loved and every time we are given the opportunity to love. We need to understand that it is perfect balance when both happen at the same time and they always can!

This is truth of such a basic and cosmic scale that it takes a while to let the absolute perfection of it sink in and work within us in its fullness of meaning. If one remembers that the basic need of all things is to love and to be loved, would one train a dog to aggressively harm others? Would one let their child always have his/her way if they got hurt by doing so, or could hurt others? Would one be abusive of others or accept abuse?

Remembering that love meets all needs and that the true need of each and every living thing is to love and to be loved can be all one needs to remember in order to make meaning in everything they do – no matter how complex it may seem. Because love wants to meet all needs, it must begin by recognizing the needs that exist. For example, a man who is 50 years old but has the mentality of a six year old cannot be expected to have the usual needs of a 50 year old man. One does not meet his needs by expecting him to behave as a 50 year old man despite the fact that he chronologically is a 50 year old man. One only meets his needs by acknowledging that he is mentally six years old and then giving him opportunities to love and to be loved at that stage of development. Only in this way, will he be able to safely grow. For only in this way will he thrive and become all he can become.

simplifying life

When we focus on the absolute truth that everyone and everything's need is to love and to be loved and that love meets all needs, we can "step outside of" the issues of the moment and stop getting caught up in day to day activities that are dualistic (not loving). For example, if you have a friend or relative that seems to need to treat you terribly, you have to at once realize that this is not their true need even if their words and actions indicate that they believe it is so. Because their only true need is to love and to be loved, and so is yours, you can solve the situation in numerous truly loving ways. One of these may be to simply articulate that you will not spend time with them until they agree to stop the behavior that is so harmful to you both.

Presenting solutions that allow you to love and to be loved and presenting the same opportunities toward others is love in action. It is no one's true need to harm others! When we stop people from being able to harm us or harm others, that is one way of being love in action.

Often, where we get clouded or confused is when we try to understand the unloving behavior. But unloving behavior is not there to be understood! It is unloving, therefore it is untruthful and not needed. Nothing more need be understood about it! All that truly needs to be understood is love. Love is the only true thing in all of existence.

We are cosmic and eternal beings. Harmful behavior can be caused by one or any combination of a number of things, all too complex for us each to figure out. Damaged upbringings, past life issues, injuries that do not allow the brain to function properly and so on, all can play a role in harmful behavior. Therefore, the only place to focus is on understanding love. Through understanding love, one can move past being affected by the harmful behavior of others and into a state of getting one's true needs met while allowing others to do the same.

It may simply be that all you need to know in a general sense is that something has happened to the person perpetrating the harmful behavior in order that they can be so separated from love and from all that they truly are. It may be that this is all you need to know in order to feel compassion for them. Compassion is love. Focusing on love and on how to be love, not on untruthful activities and their possible origins, keeps us in alignment with the energy of love instead of with the energy of non-love. This is where all answers to all questions begin.

It simplifies life to know that we do not have to understand all of the dysfunction out there. All we need to do is know what love is and understand what it does and we will navigate all the dysfunction beautifully.

Many people believe that being loving means that you will get taken advantage of or mistreated, but this belief (and this activity if it is occurring) is also based on thinking that you have to sacrifice yourself or set your own needs aside and this is never a facet of true love. The person who constantly waits on his/her mate hand and foot, doing everything for him/her while nothing is done in return, is not truly loving or being loved. He/she is not having his/her true needs met and is not meeting the true needs of his/her partner. And vice versa. "Boundaries" need to be set.

Setting boundaries only truly works if the boundaries go in place to facilitate love. In other words, if boundaries allow the possibility that love will come into what it is meant to be, then they are appropriate and only then. If the boundaries do not serve love, then they are useless and probably serve some other purpose that is not loving. Remember that love meets all needs and our true need is to love and to be loved; therefore setting boundaries has to allow being loved and loving to possibly take place.

When we think of the truth that love meets all needs; in other words, that it is encompassing and inclusive, then the ways in which we can think of to solve problems or address issues become very clear indeed. All ways that do not meet the needs of everyone and everything involved have to be set aside, for they are not from true love.

We cannot think of such solutions on our own however, and so we have to connect to the one Source that created all out of love, to love and to be loved. In other words, we have to communicate with the Source of All Love that created everything and understand that we, as physical matter in a stage of evolving in duality, require it to guide us. This is the interactive, co-creative part of the relationship between Creator and Created. This is cosmic love unfolding. This is what we are meant to do.

So many of us have forgotten this! As the time when all duality (separation) will end has approached, the illusion of separation has increased. That is because love has been growing in the physical dimension (unfortunately under the law of duality and the other laws) and as love has grown, so has all that is not love, *temporarily*. The illusion of separation from our Creator has increased to a degree where a large percentage of the human populace of this dimension have forgotten how to do something that we all have spent far more of our time doing than not: communicating with what created us!

We have spent far more time communicating with what created us than not, because much more of our existence has been spent in soul form than in physical form. In between physical incarnations, we communicate freely with Creator and we co-create freely together, all for the evolution of the love we have for one another. Not only that, but many of our past incarnations were into societies where communicating with Creator was a central precept of the society itself.

To believe that we are separate from our Creator is one of the biggest untruths in existence. To believe that our Creator is anything but love is another massive untruth. Many belief systems right now actually teach that our Creator punishes, or causes us to suffer, or deprives us of what we need and want and so on and so on. All of this is absolute untruth. Our Creator is love and only love. As truly, are we.

And here is where we can understand more about what love is by understanding what it does not do. Love never punishes. Love never causes suffering. Love does not deprive. Love does not create unloving things. In short, love does not hate!

It only becomes necessary to make what should be an obvious statement such as "love does not hate" in the face of belief systems that claim God hates! What an atrocity of duality that is! Any belief system that states that Creator hates anything, for any reason, has no true understanding of what Creator is.

Love does not hate. When love sees that something is being done that is harmful to others, it only applies love to the harm-doer in hope that the behavior will change. For love knows that only those who are not getting their true needs met (to love and to be loved) are capable of doing harm!

Love encompasses all within creation, without beginning or end. Love only loves and in so doing, creates more love. This is because love is the only truly creative force there is. Love is the only true force there is. It is only love, cosmic, eternal and in action, that has brought all of creation to the end of the time of duality and the other laws that governed that stage of our evolution and into the time of love, unified.

love, perpetuating... love, in perpetuity

Because love is our primary state of existence; that is, it is the true energy that we were created from, love is all that is real. In order to enact the types of decisions and actions that reflect this, it is necessary to understand love fully as it truly is. Where we struggle, as mentioned in the previous chapter, is that we often do not remember what love truly is.

The fact that we have become so confused in our understanding of what love is, is simply a result of the laws of existence (and in particular duality) on physical matter. This has made it difficult for people to always know how to act in ways that are true to what we are. We are the ones who exist within the duality of the physical world when we are in our bodies. When we are not in our bodies, we completely know what love is and we see our physical incarnations and our total existence in this context and in the context of what our evolution is for.

It is necessary to "look past" the dualities of this world and focus on love with this cosmic understanding, in order to do what we are truly here to do. That is when the absolute gift of connection to our Creator is the only tool we must use.

And do use, on a daily basis, multiple times a day! This connection is not some complex, mystical thing accessible only to those "in the know"! That kind of exclusivity is not love, therefore it is not truth. This connection is something each and every one of us are acting upon and connected to already, or we would not even be in existence. The question is: *how much are we aware of this connection? How much do we use it? And how much more could we use it?*

Every time you make a loving action or choice, you are in total connection to what created you. Every time you choose an action other than love, you are not. This does not mean you are alone, for Creator is always working to try to get you to come into alignment with love. What it means is that you are making choices that do not put you in alignment with what you truly are and what made you. In other words, you are not fulfilling what you are here to fulfill. Every loving choice you make is what puts you in alignment with what you are and what you are here for.

in connection to love

At this time, it is necessary to summarize what we know love is and does so far.

Love encompasses all within creation, without beginning or end. Love is only inclusive and it is inclusive of everything in existence. It does not and cannot exclude; that is, it cannot value one thing over another thing. Love does not punish or desire that something suffer, for love never harms. Love meets all needs and the only true need of everything in creation is to love and to be loved. Love only loves and in so doing, creates more love.

So we can see that the person who makes healthy foods for others and themselves is in connection to what they are and what created them. The person in traffic who is alert and does not cause an accident is in connection to what they are and what created them. The person who gives something to someone because they need and want it without feeling that they have to give up something themselves, is in connection to what they are and what created them.

These are very simple depictions, because *it is that simple*. Any time we are engaged in activities whereby everyone present gets their needs met, we are in connection to our Creator and we are allowing it to work through us. We can apply this simple concept to situations that are as big and complex as we can think of!

The clear truth that we are love and that love encompasses all and meets all needs is all we need to know to understand how to create our world. Based on that truth, a world where some people starve and some people freeze and some people die of horrible disease while others have multiple homes, multiple cars, multiple thousand dollar purses, is not a world that reflects who we are and what we were put here to do. It is a world caught up in duality, not divinity.

The belief systems that there is not enough for all, that some people don't deserve to have things, that it is a "survival of the fittest" world, do not fit with the cosmic truth of what we are and were created to be, nor with what created us. These types of belief systems – and our acceptance and enactment of them – perpetuate the energy of duality (non-love) and hold us back in our evolution into being what we truly are, as a whole creation. The good news, however, is that love, being the only true energy there is, significantly outweighs the energy of non-love throughout the cosmic energy field of creation whenever love is enacted and it is being enacted all the time.

That exactly is how we have gotten to the point in our evolution now whereby all that is not love is falling away and love is emerging as the one true energy present within all of creation: we have loved. While our bodies have not always known this, our souls always have. Our souls have tried to get our physical matter to act upon the true divine intelligence of what we are (love) and what created us (love). With great success.

Even when we have lived lives that are more unloving than loving, it is important to put those lives within the cosmic context of our entire evolution and the love that we are creating. One life out of thousands does not undo all of the love done in one's cosmic evolution across all of time. And because we are naturally loving beings, even when we don't know it and are perpetrating lives of non-love, we are also learning about love and how to be it by what it isn't and by what not to do!

Many a being upon our earth is living in peaceful and loving ways due to physical incarnations within which they learned more about what love is by learning what it is not.

You see, that is the cosmic beauty of being made of love – we learn about it and evolve into it, no matter what we do along the way.

The consciousness of creation is designed to learn! That is evolution, after all. No matter what we do, we become love in some way from it. Sometimes we become love through experiencing the effects of duality (non-love) and understanding that duality is what we don't wish to be. Sometimes we become love through experiencing the effects of love and understanding that this is what we wish to be. Sometimes we learn the hard way, with hatred. Sometimes we learn the easy way, with love. No matter what, we learn about love and we become it.

We can't do otherwise, for *we are love*. We can only be what we are.

In the period of evolution within duality and the other laws of existence, we have simply been growing the container to hold all that we are. And now we have grown it. We are moving into a new phase of evolution and this phase will be without duality (non-love) and therefore without separation from what we are and what created us.

This means that all that we have done across all of our evolution that is not love, will fall away also. All sorrow, all fear, all hatred, and so on and so on will be gone, for it is not love, therefore it is not true. It is all only a product of duality and duality was only necessary for a certain part of our evolution.

Until December 30, 2006, we had been evolving toward becoming all the love that we are. Every action, every thought that we have taken that is loving has contributed to this evolution. *Every* loving thought, *every* loving action. That is very, very empowering for it enables us to see how we each are a vital part of the entire evolution of the whole of creation. There is no such thing as a small loving action or thought. It is all magnified limitlessly in its effects upon our evolution into love.

true solutions

Because we have been evolving within duality, it has meant that we have not yet been able to create perfect loving solutions to our problems. That is okay. What has been important is to be trying or evolving toward being able to do so because in this way, we have evolved the matter that will be able to hold all the love and intelligence that we truly are. And although our solutions have not been perfect, whenever they have tried to create love they have brought us to this time when we will be able to co-create perfect loving solutions magnificently.

Let us use a concrete example. At the present time, there are millions of people around the world whom are suffering from lack of food, for a wide variety of "reasons". There is also a global awareness of this fact that was not present as recently as fifty years ago. Now there is a growing movement amongst many people to make sure others know that millions of people are starving and there is also a growing movement amongst many people to try to put in place actions that bring this lack to a halt.

The actions people are putting in place struggle against greed. They struggle against lies and corruption. They struggle against apathy and lack of will. But steadily, these actions are growing nonetheless. Why? Because they are loving.

Yes, it is true that the real answer – a loving society that does not tolerate or conceive of letting a member of it starve in a world of enough for all – has not yet come but the movement is steadily towards that end. In a few short years, the truth of how many are suffering, where and why, is coming to the attention (consciousness) of more and more people.

The new time when the intelligence of love becomes the only way things are done upon the earth means we will create the society that cannot let starvation occur. We have evolved steadily, ever since we fought as cavemen with one another over a bone (duality) instead of sharing it (love), to reach a point whereby we can actually think of and put in place such solutions.

In other words, every action and every thought that has been loving across all of time has brought us to a time where we will be able to stop starvation and other unloving events from occurring at all! We have steadily evolved our matter and consciousness until it can co-create such solutions. The end of duality means those types of loving thoughts will become action and we, as a creation, won't be able to be in duality to it!

In other words, all whom presently cause this suffering will work to bring about its end, also. We are all one, made out of love, even those amongst us who seem the most separated from this truth. Duality and the other laws of existence are the only reasons any action other than absolute love can take place at all, in any living thing and in any part of the creation.

When we look at our world and the dualities, and therefore suffering, it contains, it becomes absolutely necessary to hear and to know the truth that we are evolving toward becoming all that we are meant to be. It gives us focus. It gives us understanding. It gives us something greater than hope, for it gives us truth. When we realize that we have all been cosmically evolving, despite the illusions that keep us separated, toward the absolute perfection of all that we are, we know our own divinity and the divinity of what created us. This truth helps us to elevate out of the duality of the world around us and to know what to do next.

For now it is time to be conscious, while in physical form, of all that we are and of what we are doing. It is time to bring the time of duality and the other laws of existence that have governed creation for over 13.7 billion years to an end and enter into the age of absolute love, being what we truly are in all of the glory of what made us all.

We *are* love. *We are love.*

Therefore, we are everything that is beautiful and perfect and eternal.

It is time to create in the beauty and perfection of the love that we are and that made us. It is time to create the existence we were made to have, as a whole creation. It is time to be, while in our physical form, all that we are while in our soul form. It is time to be absolute love, loving and being loved.

the truth of being created from love

Love is the only limitless, true power that there is. It is love that created all of creation! Before creation existed, there was only love. Love is all that there was to create from and love is all that did the creating.

We were created out of love, to love and to be loved and that is the only reason we exist.

All else that exists in creation is due to the laws that were necessary to allow the energy of absolute love to become something physical. Duality is the first law. It is the law of separation that occurred because Creator, whom is only love, "divided" loveself to create us. Creator and Created. Whom are actually and truly one, in love.

Duality and the other laws of creation have governed the period of our evolution from the moment of the "big bang" (the "division") to the date of December 30, 2006. At that time, duality and the other laws reached their maximum possible level and began to dissipate before the emerging power of absolute love.

This occurred simply and only because we, as an entire creation, had reached the point in our growth where we can now contain all that love is.

How beautiful! How miraculous! How divine!

How like us and our Creator!

We are now ready to merge into the next phase of our evolution, whereby we live in absolute love, create in absolute love and do not experience separation from what we are and what created us.

In light of this truth, it is time to bring what we know when we are in our soul form, into our physical understanding.

breaking down the barriers to love

We were created to interact in love with our Creator. We were created to be love "in relation to" one another. As stated before, as love has evolved since the moment of creation, the law of duality meant that things that are not love have also developed.

This unlove has then also been applied to Creator and it has created an even greater feeling of separation – while we are in the physical world – between us and it.

The results of this duality being applied to Creator are the development of some strange belief systems indeed! And much harm to ourselves and to others because of them. We have already touched upon some of these beliefs in the previous chapters but we will address them again in this one, because we are going to focus on coming into true connection with our Creator.

Our Creator is only love. Love only loves and in so doing, creates more love. It never harms. It never values one above another for it encompasses all within it's scope and meets all needs.

Throughout human history, various belief systems (religions, sciences, politics, etc.) have come into existence that have altered the truth of what Creator is. These truths have been altered by people seeking control, seeking wealth, seeking dominance over others, etc., etc. It is like making the biggest possible "weapon" when the truth of what our Creator is becomes altered and used to cause harm!

Part of our evolution to this time, is coming to a point in our intelligence where we can see past the untruths invented by other human beings in duality and understand the truth of what created us.

A basic untrue belief that we will address now is one that states that you have to be "special" or "gifted" to communicate with Creator. This is a vital untruth to overcome, for it implies separation and it implies that some are greater than others. In truth, there are no "masters" and there are no "gurus". How can there be? We are all made out of the same thing! We are all the divine, the Created, made of cosmic eternal limitless love.

It is duality that causes human beings to categorize some things as more valuable and more gifted than others but this is not the truth of the universe. And we also have to carefully examine what such categorizations are based on. Any belief system that calls someone a "master" when they deny themselves some of the basic needs of physical existence is not a belief system based on love and the giving and receiving of all of its gifts. Any belief system that withholds truth as the privilege of a few is not a belief system based on love and the giving and receiving of all of its gifts.

And any belief system that states that "sin", guilt, punishment and suffering are a necessary or desirable part of life is not a belief system based on love and the giving and receiving of all of its gifts.

Such systems deliver messages that keep us further separated from love and from all that created us. They may even profess to speak for Creator itself, but if the message is of anything other than love, they do not. They have been founded in duality. And the time of duality has come to an end!

Each and every being in creation can communicate with Creator. Bugs do it. Horses do it and dogs. Mountains, clouds, rain, all in creation communicates with Creator. The degree to which they do so depends on how much duality is affecting them, no more and no less. For example, a horse that has been beaten and "broken" by its "owners" may not remember that it was created for the purposes of love. What's more, it may act in unloving ways itself. It has not had its primary need – to love and to be loved – met and therefore it is damaged in its behavior and its thought.

The same is true of human beings, of course! A person raised in fear-based and lack-based beliefs, may actually think that the world is full of fear and lack. Their behavior will follow accordingly. Such belief systems will affect this person and how they live their life in very dualistic ways. If they come into any position of "power" their behavior and thought could possibly affect others in unloving ways as well. If such a person ends up being part of an organization that perpetuates the same fear and lack belief system, they may even state their beliefs as though they are messages from Creator when, in fact, they are not. *Our Creator is only love.*

the simplicity of love

When creation is evolving in duality, how do we discern which messages are from Creator and which are not? How do we know what to listen to and what to believe and therefore to base our actions upon?

It is easy to discern the messages of Creator for they are the ones that are loving! They are about all of your dreams being fulfilled and all of your needs met. They are the messages about ease and joy and abundance and so on – all of which are the gifts of love. Anything otherwise, like the voice that says your dreams can't come true or that you don't deserve them to, or that you need to suffer, etc., are not messages of Creator. They come from duality. They come from untruth. They come from people who do not remember what love is and what our purpose here is. They come from a form of thinking that focuses on the physical world as though this is all there is to our existence.

Because we are part of one big being called creation, what we do and think affects us all, as one. The fear-based, lack-based thinking that is present in our world right now comes from duality. Its energetic presence is strong enough in the cosmic energy field of creation that it is definitely creating the reality of the way we live. In order to move into living in a world of truth and love, we need to challenge the untrue beliefs that are so prevalent in our thinking that they govern and create ways of living that are so untrue to what we are. We need to connect to the intelligence that is higher than the one that is feeding us the fear and lack messages. We need to connect to the cosmic love of what made us and that we are.

We need to align our belief systems into love and truth in order to create a world that embodies what we truly are.

Again, this is easy to do. *Simply put, acting and thinking only in ways that are truly loving is all we need to do.*

We have a true definition of love now: love is an energy or a force that created all out of itself, to love all and to be loved by all. Therefore, the primary need of all in creation is to love and to be loved. Love encompasses (includes) all and meets all needs. It never harms, ie; it never excludes or punishes or deprives. Love only loves and in so doing, creates more love!

Compare all belief systems to this true definition and if they are in opposition (duality) to it, then it is time to let them go and move forward into love and truth.

It is that simple.

the many gifts of love

We live in a physical world that is only just beginning to shed the effects of its evolution within the laws of duality, time, motion, space, gravity, polarity and the dimensions. As we move into the time when all will only exist and create in the unified (non-dualistic) energy of absolute love, it is time to focus on love and only on love. It is time to surmount and expel the effects of the 7 laws of existence that have made it appear, while we are in the physical dimension, that we are separated from our whole selves, from one another and from what created us.

The only way to do this is to love, purely and truly.

An understanding of what love is, purely and truly, is what we need to guide us. One of the issues we have, in this age where duality has reached its maximum possible effects, is that we try to understand ourselves and our

Creator from the point of view of duality. But that is an untruthful and illusory perspective to begin at in gaining understanding. We are love. We were made out of love. Therefore we must look to love to understand what we truly are.

We were created out of love, to love and to be loved. That is the sole (soul) reason we exist. Because we were created out of love, to love and to be loved, our only true need is to love and to be loved.

Love is the only true energy of creation. Love meets all needs. It never harms. Love only loves and in so doing, creates more love.

We are love and what created us is love.

And what we have been doing until this point in time, is evolving the physical matter that will contain all the love that we truly are.

Because duality (non-love) is not our true state, we cannot find answers to our questions, solutions to our problems and understanding of ourselves from examining it. The answers are not there. The truths are not there. They are only found in our true state, which is love.

Examining ourselves and our world from the true viewpoint that everything within it is supposed to be for love and for loving is a simple means to help us understand what we need to do in order to come into the truth of what we were created for.

Simple examples to illustrate this are easy to come up with for they exist at all levels. The previously used example about pesticides and herbicides is a very obvious one that can easily be extended to many other scenarios that have arisen during our evolution within the limits of duality and the seven laws.

Deciding what to purchase to have as possessions in one's life becomes clear when one asks this question: Does this item meet the needs of all the people whom it effects or does it have the potential to create non-love in our lives and the lives of other parts of creation? This is a big issue in this day and age as the need for love that we carry deep within ourselves has sometimes driven us, in a human society controlled by the effects of duality, to search for the means to fulfill our true need for love through whatever is readily available or marketed to us. Debt overload, debilitating stress and a global economy that does not allow for the basic needs of the many to be met are the unloving results.

Deciding what to take into oneself as a belief system becomes easier through the same question. We must ask ourselves, "Does this system of belief contain anything other than true love? Does it harm or contain the potential to harm? Does it exclude? Does it punish or blame? Does it say I need to suffer or sacrifice?" If the answer to any of those questions is yes, the belief system is not of the absolute love of our Creator, but has been created within the limits of duality (non-love). The only belief to hold is that of true love.

Overcoming such huge issues as these involves coming into one-ness with our true purpose, our true beingness, our true Creator and our true intelligence. We simply cannot solve our problems by operating within the dualistic thought processes that created them in the first place. We must remember that although duality seems to be running things right now it is only a temporary state of being, confined to the physical world, that is "on the way out". And we achieve its' demise and our rise into our true divinity, only by applying the true energy of ourselves and our Creator to its effects.

Because the new time – the time of absolute love unified and the end of duality – is happening right now, this becomes about being in alignment with it as it unfolds. The new time is happening. It is here. It is now occurring for all of creation. For human beings, as the most complex part of the creation with the most complex issues, understanding what is happening and what tool is needed (love) and how to use it to come into alignment with the truth of what all of creation is, means that human beings will be able to move with the change much more easily than if they cling to the illusions of duality and the other laws.

For as the unified energy of absolute love permeates all of creation (which is what it is steadily doing right now and has been doing since December 30, 2006) duality and all that it has created and controls, will not be able to be sustained. We are seeing much evidence of this already. Indeed, the inventions of duality have never stood the test of time. By their very nature, being not eternal, they cannot. This itself is why, throughout our long evolution, empires and belief systems, leaders and inventions have disappeared. If they were not formed in absolute love, they are unsustainable.

all that love is

The new time, when love will become the only energy permeating all of creation, began on December 30, 2006.

Because of this, the energy of love becoming unified as duality falls away is spreading throughout the cosmic energy field. The cosmic energy field is a term invented to describe the energy of our one-ness as a whole creation. Therefore it includes everything in creation. The part of this cosmic energy field (sometimes called the collective consciousness, the matrix or the grid, etc.) that is human beings is the most complex, because human beings are the most complex part of the creation.

As a creation, we are comprised of the simple and the complex. Both are necessary for the creation to be complete and, in keeping with the encompassing love it is made of, both are of equal value. However, the more complex parts of the cosmic energy field hold more of the illusion of duality or separation and therefore are the slowest to respond to the energy of the energy field as it changes. The simple parts of creation hold the least duality. They respond quickly to the cosmic energy field as it changes and they are often where the changes begin that move all of creation forward into becoming absolute love.

But creation is all one thing! The magnificence of all that love is and how it encompasses all within it, means that the parts of the creation that merge into the energy of the pure love of the new time first will, through the cosmic energy field that binds us all as one, take the rest of creation with them!

So air and light and vibration and water and weather and so on and so on, are all coming into the absolute love state of the new time. And this energy has been filtering steadily to all of the rest of the creation.

This differs from the prediction of the new time, although all prediction of the new time and all of the work we have done as a whole creation is how we have attained it. How this differs is that we are no longer trying, striving and growing toward what we are, we are actually *becoming* it and then *being* it. It is without question. It is without doubt. It is without possibility of setback. It is growing steadily in its energetic presence within creation. It is becoming, now and forever, the wholeness of the absolute love we truly are, without duality.

In other words, there is nothing any of us can do about it, other than go with it! This is the promise we were created to fulfill, coming into fulfillment: We are love and we will be all that love is, now. The purpose of this book is to raise awareness and understanding of what really is occurring, so that we can all consciously help it along faster, at all levels of creation, simple and complex.

Through this awareness and this understanding, we are each able to work within our part of the cosmic energy field to facilitate the new time of love without duality into becoming faster! We are helping to bring about the world of absolute love we were created to be, faster. We are being a part of the true change we know our world needs to undergo. We are ending the illusion of separation from all the love that we are and all the love that created us, to love us and to be loved by us.

All of creation has been in a journey of evolution into being what we truly are. This journey has occupied just over 13.7 billion years of time. But because of the law of time itself, that phase of our evolution is now over. Every loving act and every loving thought we have ever made – as the whole of creation – has brought us here, now. Now we are only to be it.

We can become active in employing the cosmic energy field to end duality and bring the time of love we all yearn for into being. This is a powerful tool – in the true sense of the word power which is love – that has always been instrumental in bringing us to where we are now, in our evolution as a whole. As mentioned before, the energy of duality seems to be controlling the cosmic energy field right now. In truth, it is only if you think human beings are all that matter in creation that you can actually believe that duality is in control! The most complex part of creation has been creating complex illusions of duality, that have been spilling over and affecting the less complex parts of it, indeed.

However, it is the most simple parts of the creation, responding to the true energy of absolute love in the cosmic energy field, that are shifting this. They are holding the energy of this absolute love and steadily, steadily, changing the complex parts of the energy field of all of creation. Human beings are coming awake to what they are in ways never before seen! All that is needed now is to empower human minds as part of the cosmic energy field, to the full truth of what is going on, without duality.

That is the function, ultimately, of this writing. To bring *us*, as human beings, into true awareness of what is already occurring, so we, too, can help it to come about.

In other words, the new time is not about the "end of the world" or any other dualistic messages that are out there in the human portion of the cosmic energy field right now.

This is about absolute truth. This is about love, fulfilled. This is about love, as it was made to be. This is about love, as it is.

The time of duality is over.

The time of love has begun.

thoughts of love

Because we are all part of what is known as the cosmic energy field, we have the incredible ability to help the cosmic energy field – and therefore all of creation – come into the absolute love of the new time through the power of our truly co-creative thoughts. Indeed, the cosmic energy field is the major way we have evolved together as a whole creation until now. Because we have been co-creating our evolution into love ever since the moment we were created, we have been using the cosmic energy field in its most true way ever since we began. Yes, duality energy has permeated it also, but as already articulated, that has only ever been a temporary state of existence.

We help the energy of duality to end by loving and only by loving. When we make choices founded on the absolute truth of love, when we share the absolute true definition of love with others in creation, when we invent using the guidance of absolute love, we are being our divinity and co-creating with our Creator. In other words, when we use the energy of our physical matter and our thoughts (consciousness) to make truly loving acts happen, we are being true co-creators. More and more, this is occurring throughout creation, including within the most complex part of it; humankind. There are people everywhere now who, through their connection to the absolute truth of Creator, have co-created solutions to the problems duality has presented to our existence. They have solutions that meet the criteria of absolute love. That is, these solutions meet the needs of all in creation as they are enacted and cause absolutely no harm to anyone or anything.

The people with the true solutions know how they got them, too! They know they did not "think them up on their own". They know they are a part of the Creative Source – whatever moniker they give it – that has co-created the perfect solution with them and they know that this Creative Source is love. What now is to be done, as a whole creation, is to disband the machinery of duality that has prevented these solutions from being enacted and bring love into being as we were created to do.

How do we do that?

We do that through loving thought and through loving action and through loving connection to what we truly are and to what made us, the way we have done everything loving and true throughout our entire co-creative evolution!

Through the conscious decision to love and to only love and through putting the energy of this conscious decision into the cosmic energy field, we will change the world while it is changing us as we always have; only this time we will be changing it into the unified energy of absolute love without duality. Remember that this is happening anyway – our Creator is already bringing the time of love about with the less complex parts of creation that have heard and connected to this unified energy. This is promise fulfilled. This is love, coming into being love in its absolute form. What this is about, for humankind, is drawing the absolute power of love into our being consciously and emitting the absolute power of love consciously into the rest of creation through our thoughts, words and deeds as the less complex parts of the creation are already beginning to do.

This is beautiful because it is as simple as knowing what to focus our portion of the cosmic energy field on (through our thoughts and actions) and helping it to grow.

We are love. We are cosmic eternal love.

All that is to be done, is to know it and to be it, while in our bodies as in our souls.

After all, effective December 30, 2006, we finished evolving the matter that would hold this cosmic eternal love. It took just over 13.7 billion years to evolve all of that matter but, because duality is not our true state, it will take only about one human generation to be finished with it!

Through focusing on the true power of love, we and our Creator are what will "change the world". Through connecting to what we truly are and what created us, we will bring about the next phase of our evolution, that of evolving without the energy of duality (non-love).

our souls are love

Begin by acting as your soul does. Your soul is love. Within your life, as it exists now, begin to focus love on everything it contains. Love your furniture for being part of your comfort, love your food for feeding you, love the people you are with and the materials that surround you and form your environment. Love your body for being the vessel that holds your magnificent soul and the bodies of others for the same reason. Give the energy and intention of love to everything you already have in your life.

If anything causes you feelings of non-love, change it in some way so that it causes you feelings of love. For example: If the expensive car in the driveway keeps you awake at night wondering how you can pay for it and heat the house, perhaps it is time to trade it in for one that lets you do both and sleep. Let it go, with love, and know that you have begun to live in a way that allows love in. From love comes all the gifts of creation that we truly need. At some point in time, that may include an expensive car but right now may not be the time, while it is generating non-love energy in your life. In fact, it may be interfering with your ability to move forward into the energy of absolute love.

Next, begin focusing your future choices of what to bring into your life and what to put into the lives of others so that they include only the definition of what love truly is. Give every choice in your life the true energy of love. Ask Creator, who created you, to help you bring love more fully into your life. The beauty of all of this is that it is a circle. The more you strive to be what you are, the more you will be it. The more you focus on love, the more love comes in. The more you focus on connection with what created you, the more Creator can work in your physical matter to bring about true connection with it, as you have when you are in your soul unencumbered by a dense and complex form of matter.

Remember what the true definition of love is.

We were created out of love, to love and to be loved. That is the sole (soul) reason we exist. Because we were created out of love, to love and to be loved, our only true need is to love and to be loved.

Love is the only true energy of creation. Love meets all needs. It never harms. Love only loves and in so doing, creates more love.

We are love and what created us is love.

Therefore, our sole (soul) purpose is to love and to be loved.

When we look at every aspect of our lives from this viewpoint, so much clarity is gained. If something in our life is not for love, we must alter things so that it is or so that non-loving energy is not present in our lives or the lives of those we effect. If something we want has the possibility of creating non-love for ourselves or others, we must choose otherwise.

It matters not where we are in life. If we have no home or no possessions, focusing on loving and being loved opens the door to getting what we need. Sometimes it is hard, yes. If you are the one starving or being abused, definitely duality is affecting you a great deal and much of it without your own choice! But connection to Creator and knowing that love will find the true solution is the only place to begin in overcoming the duality that is governing your existence.

We live in a world where much exists that does not choose love for ourselves and others. It is absolutely true that we have the power to change this and the power is love. *Love only loves and in so doing creates more love.* Begin by asking Creator to help you in applying love to the immediate things you have to face – ie: the things you have in your life based on how they affect yourself as a part of the whole of creation. As this understanding and enactment of love is used and grows, your ability to be part of bigger loving solutions will also grow. Remembering our example about the fifty year old man with the mental ability of a six year old, begin where you are at. Chalk up past "mistakes" and traumas to the period of our evolution known as the time of duality and move into the time of love.

connecting with love

Let's use another example to illustrate how love has the power to change the universe and everything within it into absolute love. This example expands the concept into the miracles that can occur when we truly understand what we are and what created us.

Let's say you love coffee. Now let's say that you have become aware that coffee is one of the most pesticided crops grown in the world. Let's also say that you now know that market demand for coffee, grown with unloving methods, is causing the depletion of the vital rainforests upon which much of our earth's air supply depends.

So right now, we are realizing that the consumption of coffee under these circumstances is not very loving at all. However, the gifts of the world are intended to truly be the gifts of love! How can you enjoy the coffee you love in a loving way?

Coffee, organically grown in the shade of the rainforest addresses many of those issues of non-love that we identified. Choosing to purchase coffee that is grown in this way is very loving. As human beings have evolved closer and closer to the time when duality will end, they have begun to realize and search out such loving solutions in larger numbers. In other words, they are seeking solutions that are more loving within a world of duality. But because we are yet living with the effects of duality, the consumption of coffee still contains duality. For example: it is shipped using means that emit harmful substances into the environment we all occupy.

This problem seems insurmountable to our limited intelligence. It seems insurmountable because we see how complex the issue of having a cup of coffee in a loving way has become! But that is only true if we have not yet learned to connect fully with Creator who always has a loving solution. By connecting with this intelligence we begin to get the cosmic solutions we were incapable of thinking of and enacting within the limits of the physical world.

These solutions begin with understanding that love is the only true power that there is. When we "harness" the power of love, vast, eternal and miraculous, and create more love with it, our solutions are nothing short of miraculous, for they have the power to alter dualistic physical matter and change it into love!

Connecting with Creator so the two of you can put love into the emissions formed by the transportation carrying the coffee and turn them into love that flows into the atmosphere replenishing it, is one example of what Creator will present to you as a solution. Or just simply asking Creator to connect with you and suffuse all of the coffee industry with love so that it can continue to evolve into all that it truly is, is enough. The point is to let the miraculous and divine love of our Creator and you create the miracle of healing and unifying yet another aspect of our creation into love, at all levels.

How does this work, you wonder? How can this be?

First of all, as you know when you are in your soul form, this can be because all is created out of love. Love is all that there is, after all! Love is the only limitless energy there is! It is duality (non-love) in action as a limited and limiting energy that has caused harmful products to be created out of what is in existence in the physical dimension. But all in existence is actually only created out of love in the first place. The power of giving those things the intent of absolute love is enough to shift them!

This is the true solution to what is needed in our world. This is the comprehension of what love is, in its truest and purest state and this is putting it into action to do the miracles that only it can do.

All we need to do is get rid of the limits of our own physical consciousness, releasing the dualistic barriers it contains to what we truly are, to what created us, and to what love is, in order to do this!

And how do we get rid of these barriers?

We get rid of these barriers by asking our Creator who created us to come fully into our bodies bringing all that our soul is with it and help us to know what we truly are.

We get rid of these barriers by asking to be all the love that we truly are, without duality.

We get rid of these barriers by consciously taking actions like the ones above and seeing what love does, as it grows and dispels the limits of duality! And as it grows and dispels the limits of duality, the miracles it does will only grow and increase themselves. Through thinking this and doing it, you will experience it.

the intent of love

Everything we create has only the intent we give it. If we intend it for love, it causes no harm. The problem, as stated in the earliest parts of this writing, is that we have not fully understood what love is while we have been surrounded by the duality of the physical dimension. The problem is that we have not focused the intent of love on so many of the things we have invented and the energy of duality has been present within them instead.

Love is the pure energy that created all! It is the only truly creative energy there is. The beautiful statement, already articulated, that when we create in love, we are creating with our "divine intelligence" versus our dualistic one, is perfect to repeat here.

Love is the pure energy that created all! Because love is capable of creating nebulas, oceans, galaxies and so on and so on, why would it not be capable of breaking pollution down into its elementary forms and restoring them to their original loving energetic state?

We are the limiting thinking, here. We, in our limited and dualistic world, have only just grown up enough to comprehend that we are meant to be a part of something that enacts miracles of love throughout creation. We have only just grown up enough to comprehend all that we truly are and are part of.

Notice that the words are: "part" of something that enacts miracles of love. For the only way we can do this is by working hand in hand with what created us.

Where we fail in that connection, we will fail in creating miracles.

Come to know Creator for what Creator is.

In this way and only in this way you will come to know yourself!

Evolve your intelligence past the limited and dualistic definitions that others in the physical world where duality and limits exist, have told you and are telling you Creator is, and come to know it as the miraculous eternal love that it is!

Only in this way will you be able to enact the sort of miracles that defy the present human mind (limited as it is). Only in this way will you be able to be part of totally transforming the universe and our world within it into the place it was meant to be, where only loving action occurs.

You need not worry, however. This time in our evolution is being and is going to be, whether you actively take action at this time or not. Those who "get it" and can take part in it now, will simply take all with them, as part of the whole. But how grand – and how truly loving – it is for all to help all!

If you can think it, it can happen. Thought, after all, is the original creative act and thoughts are energy! When your thoughts are of love, all of the rest of creation and Creator help you to bring it about! Whether it is dissolving the liquids that aircraft spreading "chem-trails" are issuing into the environment so that they can cause no harm, changing the minds of people who create non-food substances that harm brain matter, adding healing energy to the foods you consume, or manifesting something you need in your life to create love with, if you align yourself with all the love that you truly are and all the love that made you, all you can do is miracles of absolute love.

It is the knowing of this and the doing of this, that now needs to occur in the physical human being. We need to understand the power of love and the power of thought and use it as we were meant to.

We are divine love, created out of the divinity of love. We have always been this. This is what we are. It is only our physical matter, in a state of evolution, that has not been able to comprehend the fullness of what this means. The new time unfolding on the earth is about knowing what we are and being it, as a whole creation.

Even those who exist deep within duality, disconnected from the trueness of love, from the truth of what they are and even twisting the truth of what the Creator is, will be part of this transformation of all of creation! How can they not be? They exist! Therefore they are a part of creation and truly they are made of love. You are now a part of the energy of the new time, just with reading these words. Use the love power of all that you are when joined together with our Creator, and help those disconnected from their own divinity to remember what they are by sending them thoughts of love. This is how we will change the world.

all you need is...

Everything in creation was made out of love. That is, love is the primary energy from which all was created. However, duality and the other laws have made it seem as though something other than love exists. Duality and the other laws of existence, put in place for a temporary period of time to allow energy to become physical matter, have made it seem as though love has opposites.

This energy that is oppositional to love has much presence right now, within our physical world. However, we cannot heal duality by applying duality. If that were true, war would have solved the problem of war long ago, the application of toxic chemicals would have healed cancer instead of increasing its occurrence and so on. The only way to heal duality is through love. Love is the only true power there is.

Duality and the other laws only exist within the physical dimension. When we or anything in creation is in soul form, these laws do not affect us. That is when we understand it all: our Creator of love, our origins of love and our evolution into love.

Shedding the layers of duality our physical matter holds is easy, for that is not what we truly are. Although we, as a whole creation, took 13.7 billion years to evolve until this time, we will shed our duality within a generation. Human beings have been a physical part of evolution for only 4.7 million years although the energy that would become human beings was created at the same time as everything else in the big bang. However, as the most complex part of the creation, human beings have been affected the most by duality and the other laws.

Shedding the layers of duality our physical matter holds is easy: All we have to do is move into loving communication with our Creator and ask for it to be removed now because it is time. The more we do this asking, and the more the duality we have accumulated is removed, the more we move into the true energy of the love that we are.

Communicating with Creator involves understanding that we were created out of it and that it is love. Because love wants to meet all needs and our only true need is to love and to be loved, this need we are expressing will be met. As duality leaves our physical bodies in the new time that is unfolding, the energy of love that our soul is – and a fuller connection to our Source of creation – will come into them more and more.

This is the first time we are able to do this since the moment of the big bang! This is the time we have been waiting and evolving toward since that first moment of our creation: when our physical matter had evolved enough to hold all that we truly are. The hard work is done. We have now only to help it unfold and encompass us all fully, by being what we truly are.

Love is far more natural to what we truly are, than hate is! Communicating with what created us and co-creating with it is much more natural to what we are as well. Sometimes, just simply getting "our heads around" the concept is all we need to proceed with ease. What you are is love and it is time to be what you are! And so it will simply unfold.

Where we slow it down is by staying mired in duality, as though it is real. If we cling to unloving ideas, simply because we have them in our physical matter and do not let love and truth in, our journey into the new time will be slower and more disrupted. If we align ourselves with the truth of creation and with our Creator, if we access the power of love and actively carry out its truth, we will help all of us to come into the new time with much more ease.

love, applied

Applying the true definition of love to everything is all we need to do. Again, we cannot find answers to our problems by striving to understand the duality that created them and that they operate within. What we must do is focus on understanding and being love, on applying love and communicating with love and from this, the answers to all problems will naturally arise and in more miraculous and more encompassing ways than we could have ever imagined!

We were created out of love, to love and to be loved. That is the sole (soul) reason we exist. Because we were created out of love, to love and to be loved, our only true need is to love and be loved.

Love is the only true energy of creation. Love meets all needs. It never harms. Love only loves and in so doing, creates more love.

Again, let's work with a few examples to see how this can be practically applied to our lives as they exist and as we are evolving into the time of love.

We will work our way through a broad range of problems and solutions, encompassing everything from the "every day" life of individuals to issues of global concern, keeping in mind that not one of these issues is trivial within the cosmic scale of what we are doing in our evolution. What truly matters within each one, is that love be enacted in creating the solution.

We begin by relaying the story of a woman who we will call "Sue". Sue works teaching children. She works with many others whose job is to do the same. One of her co-workers, however, is cruel to the children, speaking disparagingly to them and about them. She is putting a whole lot of negative and non-loving energy into the children and into the workplace and it is generating lots of non-loving scenarios. Sue has tried to intervene, spreading love to the children by hugging them and by setting things right again with comforting and truthful words. She has even spoken to the co-worker on more than one occasion, with kindness and understanding. But the behavior is not changing and in fact, it is getting worse. This causes Sue great distress and she lays awake at night pondering a dilemma: Should she report this woman to their supervisory body?

This type of situation arises in our society on a daily basis. Whether it is the person who should not be driving for whatever reasons, the child who hits other children on the playground when unsupervised or the co-worker who does not do his/her job, when we apply the truth that our only need is to love and to be loved, we can immediately shed clarity on things. Complex, multi-layered problems may require applying the simple definition of love to each complex layer until we solve the whole problem through and through, meeting all needs.

The fact we must begin with, in helping Sue enact in love and truth, is that this whole situation is bigger than she is alone. Although she is acting in a very loving way, it is not changing the situation rapidly enough. Where she must begin is by asking Creator to help her to fill the entire situation with love for a loving outcome to be provided for all involved. We are never alone, ever. All we need to do is know that and ask the love that created us to help us with our problems in ways that reflect what we truly are and what made us.

This was always true even before coming to the end of duality, for this is the only way we have been able to evolve enough to get here. Our Creator's love for every part of the creation is vast and eternal! Letting it into every situation by asking it to use us as a vessel or instrument of its vast and eternal love is where every truly loving solution must begin.

Next we ask the question: Is "to love and to be loved" taking place in the scenario above? This question has to be applied to every player in the entire scenario to be answered properly. The children are not being loved by this woman; nor are they being provided with the opportunity to be loving for they have grown to dislike her intensely. This woman is not being loving nor is she being loved. In fact, absence of love in her entire life is the culprit for her behavior in the first place! She does not know what love is, nor how to enact it, nor how to get it! And certainly, Sue is not being loved in this case either – laying awake at night pondering such a big problem is not receiving love.

Asking Creator to help her to put the energy and intention of cosmic love into the scenario and being willing to be a vessel of that love gave Sue a surprising answer. She realized that she had been explaining something to someone that had no ability to understand it based on life experience. Therefore, Sue and God decided to try creating that experience for the co-worker first. This fit well also with what made Sue feel happy and at peace in her heart. She began to leave gifts, unsigned but with messages like "You are loved", coupled with magazine articles about how to deal with children, stress and so on on the woman's desk. Whatever messages Creator guided her to, she used.

Some of the gifts, articles and sayings Sue was guided to made no discernible sense to her, other than that they were loving. She herself felt Creator's love for her and for the other person increasingly as time went on. She felt herself growing, becoming wiser, stronger and more connected. Her own feelings of loneliness began to dissipate. She could feel more and more purpose coming into her own life. Her own gifts of creativity and of love were becoming more clear.

While this was going on, Sue looked into the repercussions of reporting her co-worker. She discovered that if the woman was reported, she would most likely receive a paid stress leave and some counselling. Together with Creator, Sue sent intent to this loving outcome that would meet the needs of both the woman and the children.

In a short while, Sue did see some pretty amazing changes in her co-worker! She could see and hear the changes in the woman's voice and the woman began to take care of herself through the introduction of better foods, more flattering clothes and so on. She also began to be much much more positive toward the other adults she worked with. The changes were wonderful but they were not enough to lay Sue and Creator's deep and very real concerns for everyone involved to rest. Asking Creator to guide her so that every word was love and truth, she sent a letter to the supervisory board.

Sue continued to work with Creator as a vessel to bring absolute love into the scenario. She knew the problems were too complex for herself to figure out so being a vessel of the eternal love that could was the only true solution. A short time later, the woman was granted a stress leave of one year. Unbeknownst to Sue, several parents had already written letters of angry complaint and the supervisory board was considering its options. The letter she crafted, as a caring co-worker, was enough to direct them in enacting the perfect solution!

Sue understood that she had played a role in helping this woman to feel loved for the first time ever and even to directing her in what path to take during her stress leave through the gifts and messages from Creator that she had been a vessel of! She kept sending love to this woman and asking Creator to bring it all to a happy outcome. During that year, the woman received counselling for depression and for coping with her alcoholic husband. She also realized that teaching children was not her vocation – the thought of returning to it filled her with stress – so she received training for another job and moved on with much more happiness than she had ever had before, because she was becoming who she truly is. The woman who filled her teaching position also had her needs – for full-time employment she loved close to her home – fully met.

Sue understood something profoundly true in this case: her own true need is to love and to be loved. She knew that she herself could only be a part of a solution that brought this about and so the actions she took toward the co-worker, every step of the way, had to be about that for herself also. She took each step hand in hand with Creator, and was a part of miracles unfolding on a daily basis! The end result for Sue? Her loving letter to the supervisory board led to her being offered a position in the human resources department mediating between the board and workers, with a two-fold increase in pay! In this way, someone using their love connection with Creator had the opportunity and position to use it to increase the love in the lives of many!

As the time of love begins, Sue is taking all of this a step farther. She is asking Creator to flow through her as a vessel of eternal love, healing whatever is needed to be healed in her corner of the world. She has been part of incredible miracles of love and giving – everything from programs that feed hungry children in her large urban area, to programs that get kids off of drugs. All of these miracles happen with great ease. For most of them, Sue isn't even a physical attendee! She simply, through hearing and working with Creator, puts cosmic eternal thoughts of love truly meeting all needs into a scenario and sooner or later, she finds out about the results!

Now, together, Sue and Creator are moving into applying this loving concept into global issues. And Creator is beginning to get Sue to understand how the two of them can focus this love as energy into the cosmic energy field of all of creation in general so that the message and understanding of the time of love will grow within it faster and all will know they are loved.

turning duality into love

Our Creator looks after all needs, including those we cannot even perceive we have due to the limits of our dualistic intelligence. But if we focus on being an embodiment of true love in action, co-creating solutions with our Creator, only love and love and love is the result.

Love only loves and in so doing, generates more love. That is what love is and that is what love does.

Until the time of the end of duality, sometimes the love we have given has only had its repercussions fully known when we reach soul form or even into our next incarnation! But that also is love in action as the only eternal force there is! Love cannot be limited to one incarnation, or one moment or event!

Our souls know this. Our souls are this. We and our Creator are cosmic, eternal love.

Let's move into another example.

There is a very polluted lake in Africa, where some human beings unlovingly dumped some very very toxic waste, the by-products of modern day war. This lake has become very contaminated, to the point where the water is not drinkable and it seems as though life within it is negligible.

But within this lake is a form of fish, very ancient and simple in its composition and function. This fish is what is called a "bottom feeder"; over time, its role has been to clean the lake bed. When this toxic waste was dumped into the lake, many forms of life within it died for they could not withstand the effects of the poisons. However, this particular fish and some other simpler life forms not only survived the toxic saturation, they actually adapted to it. Being simple, less dualistic life forms means these fish understood Creator when it asked them to join with it to enact as beings co-creating the opportunity for love to take place and do its' miracles. Because they can withstand the pollution, their population has multiplied unopposed and their numbers have reached staggering proportions and each and every one of these fish is busy cleaning up the lake! In three short years, some other forms of life have returned to the lake because it supports them again.

This is love in action, cosmic and eternal. All over the earth, in polluted and damaged places, the same thing is happening. Bodies of water populated only by certain forms of algae or mussels or jellyfish that can withstand the toxicity, are being cleaned up and restored to health by them so that other forms of life (and therefore of love) can return.

Within contaminated soils, simple organisms that are all that can survive are helping the soils to return to a state of being love and supporting life again. These simple forms have far less barriers to the energy of eternal love that they are both comprised of and that is directing them to restore the well-being of the earth we inhabit as a part of the whole of creation.

The same is true of simple-celled viruses and bacteria. Human beings, creating "solutions" through dualistic means, have attempted to eradicate these organisms outright due to an incomplete understanding of what they do for all of creation. Now these viruses and bacteria are mutating rapidly, trying to become able to eradicate the very chemicals that are capable of eradicating them and hence all of the population of the earth, yourself included!

But, people say, these viruses and bacteria kill us! Yes, that negative event happens and when it does, all of creation and Creator is deeply, deeply saddened. But it does only happen to a very very very minute portion of creation and then only if they are engaged in living in unloving ways that do not foster their bodies' abilities to compatibly live with these organisms. The Bubonic plague only occurred due to the inappropriate handling of human and animal feces within a highly populated area.

And to this day there are still people who choose to forcibly inject poisonous chemicals as well as viruses into themselves in order to "protect" themselves from viruses – a strange cycle of dualistic thinking if ever there was one! And other people do not do the simple, non-harmful act of lovingly washing their hands after using the washroom!

This is duality in action. Let us turn it into love, with every choice, including those we make in public restrooms and help the simpler forms of creation co-create the world we were truly intended to inhabit. Consciously. Actively.

For the simpler forms of creation know that we are all cosmic and eternal. They know what we are working toward and they know we will all get there together, for we are one thing. For some parts of the creation, it may mean they have to go through another life cycle or even two to "catch up" with what the simpler aspects are knowing and enacting! But the end result is the same: We are made out of love and love is what we will be.

More and more, the energy of the end of duality is coming to the "attention" of the simpler components of creation and this energy is building and building, taking all with it. This writing is a message that enables us all to be an active part of it, to move out of duality and into love, cosmic and eternal, with it. It is a message of love, from our Creator to us.

love, eternal

We have spoken of the simple life forms and how they are able to adapt to withstand unloving action and bring about love again. They are working with their cosmic, divinely connected intelligence as they do so. What we have to understand, as human beings, is the fact that everything on earth and throughout the universe was created out of love, to love and to be loved. Therefore everything has a purpose our dualistic intelligence cannot always understand. Yet.

Because everything was created out of love, to love and to be loved, this is what it will become. In the meantime, duality (all that is not love) has affected it. This means that the very viruses, bacteria, weather currents, etc. that are capable of keeping our entire ecosystem functioning at levels we do not understand, also have the capability to kill or harm some other forms of life. This will no longer happen after duality ends.

Because everything will be unified into the true energy with which it was created, nothing will any longer be able to cause harm. Everything will only be able to meet all needs. Everything will only be able to love and in so doing, create more love.

We need to understand that all of this is only truly able to occur through our true and full connection to our Creator because this is what we have been created to love and to be loved by! As we struggle as a creation through the days of duality and the other laws, sometimes we have not remembered this. Forgetting this basic truth and letting duality get in the way of the truth of what we are and what created us, is the only way we can both be harmed and can harm others in creation.

As in everything we do, when we are working to help others to come to healing this connection is vital! True healing only occurs through this connection. People who work as healers (whether in modern medicine, "new age" practices, education and so on) that do not work with Creator are not doing true healing. Because they are not doing true healing, their ability to potentially harm some part of creation is very high.

Let's use the example of energy-healing the land. Because everything is energy, this is a particularly easy one to illustrate the point with and it is a personal co-experience of ours (Christine with Creator).

absolute love heals absolutely

Throughout human history, people have invented ways to cleanse the energy of unloving (dualistic) activity from the energy field of the earth itself. This is a truly loving intention to have! However, doing it without our Creator connection severely limits the true healing impact this beautiful intention has. If we do not work with Creator, the best we can do is eliminate some of the negative energy or disperse it to other places. This dispersement of energy, which of course responds to the seven laws, can have results not understandable by our present physical intelligence.

Recently, some people with partially right intent (the intent can only ever be completely right if it involves connection with Creator) attempted to heal a piece of land emanating some very negative energy. This energy was so negative that very little vegetation grew on the land, very few animals travelled there and people who came to it felt unbelievably sad or else fought with one another. The people who had come to heal the land had learned some rituals and tools of land healing with energy and so they called upon the energy field to help them, as they had been taught at the course they attended. This is not the tool to use if one wishes to do true healing, for the energy field contains much duality! It can hardly be used to heal dualistic energy from the land or from other people.

In the days of duality, if you do not specify that you wish Creator's absolute love to work with you and if you draw on anything other than Creator, the possibility of getting energy that is dualistic (non-loving in its intent) is very very likely. The people who worked on the aforementioned piece of land had many tools, but none of them were the truly right one! All they succeeded in doing was moving the negative energy and dividing it into parts. Some of this negative energy went into the portion of the energy field of one of the people involved, who has been incredibly ill ever since. Some went higher up into the mountains and began affecting land there. And some landed right in the middle of the neighbouring highway. Roadkill and car accidents were the result within hours.

This is a very glaring example of how our failure to remember and to use our connection to our Creator, who is the source of absolute love that can do no harm, can have can have very negative results for ourselves and many other parts of creation. Nothing was healed in this exercise. In fact, more negative energy was perpetrated!

It is only through connecting to our Creator fully and being a willing vessel of its love that we have ever been able to heal anything, live fully, love truly or evolve forward into the end of duality, throughout our entire evolution. This is because total connection is what we were created for, to enact in love with.

As the time of duality unfolds, we will cease to have to ask for this connection to occur every time we need it because we will truly be one with what created us. It is only within duality that we need to be very very attentive to this connection and to articulating it as part of our true intention of love! As the most complex part of the creation, with the most effects of duality impacting them, human beings must be sure to use this tool in every walk of life.

In fact, this is the only tool you need! Rituals of any form are only as good as their meaning! Unless you love them and focus on their meaning as connection to Creator, they can be utterly dispensed with when one understands that all one needs to do is ask to be a vessel of Creator's divine love in everything one does! This is the only way miracles occur.

True miracles are the ones that enact all the trueness of love, for all involved, everywhere and at every moment. Clearly there is only one Source of the type of intelligence that can understand this and carry it out. Until the time of love is completed and duality is gone, we need to consciously connect to this Source for all truly loving outcomes to take place.

But we also have to understand that Creator cannot do it without us! Without us being willing vessels of bringing our Creator's absolute love to the physical world, it does not happen. This is the other part of "to love and to be loved". This is being active co-creators. We have been active co-creators of our evolution all the way along and being aware of this beautiful soul truth while in our bodies is how we bring the new time of absolute love into fullness throughout all of our physical creation.

After this event, understanding that it is only through connection with Creator that true healing occurs, we (Christine & Creator) went on a beautiful trip into the mountains. The land mired under this type of negative energy could not "hear" Creator itself. Being a willing and consciously active co-creator of true healing with Creator, we had worked with applying the true definition of love to my (Christine's) life and eradicating the effects of duality from my (Christine's) physical matter. Although this work is not yet done of course, together, we were able to bring enough of Creator's absolute love into this situation to not only lift the negative energy entirely out of all the places it had settled, but also so that the mountain itself was awakened to the time of love and understands it fully. The mountain has begun to use its connection with Creator to unify the energy fields and matter of all of the mountains around it with the energetic message that the new time has begun. The clouds that pass over the mountain top also receive this true co-creative message and spread the energy of the end of duality wherever they go, using their own conscious Creator connection!

For everything in creation is one thing, made of love! Everything in creation is part of the cosmic energy field. Everything in creation has consciousness. This consciousness differs from the consciousness of human minds – for one thing, it is less complex and therefore duality affects it less – but it is still consciousness and this consciousness can be love or not love. This is why it is so very very important to love the things you have in your life. In giving them the conscious awareness that they are for love and for being loved, you change the very energetic presence of the things you own so that they also evolve out of duality!

It is through this united love that we (Creator and Christine) are able to heal the vehicle we drive so that its emissions are no longer harmful and it will not leave the driveway if there is anything that needs attending to in its function. As its consciousness comes into the fullness of being loved and being loving, it articulates what it likes and wants done in its care. It also gives loving reminders about what has been forgotten or where it would like to travel. Through the connection of the vehicle to Creator, Creator and it are working on getting it to the point where it no longer will require fuel to run it at all!

All over this physical dimension, there are elements, animals, things and people who are understanding these kinds of concepts and working with Creator to end duality and give everything the perfect energy of the absolute love of the new time. For all of creation is becoming what it is created to be: love absolutely.

And as the time of love absolute and without duality unfolds, creation and Creator will continue to evolve! For love is without beginning and love is without end. Love is the only truly creative force there is. It is just that as duality falls away, nothing will be able to be created that contains duality. All that will be created will only be able to be love for the purposes of love. Our Creator is a creative being, therefore, so is creation! How many ways can be created that can express all that love is? Especially when love is never ending in its evolution?

our true purpose

Because love is the primary energy of all in existence, freeing ourselves of the dualistic limits to love that our physical matter contains involves seeing all that we are as a means to be an enactment of love, loving and being loved. Right now, in the physical world, there exist human beings who invent things capable of great harm to other parts of creation, but when the incredible gifts of invention these people contain become free of such duality, think of the amazingly loving things they will create!

It is the same of every single being within creation and every single ability, talent and so on, that they contain. All that we are only gains true value if we put it to loving intent. All that we are and have is only to be used for love.

From the despotic world leader with the ability to rally people en masse, to the military strategist, to the inventor of a pharmaceutical drug: take the duality (non-love) out of their abilities and use them for love and they will become perfect.

This is what the new time will be: a time when everyone and everything, every idea, every concept, every ability, will be for the trueness of love and only for love. This is what we have been created to be, after all. This is what we are created out of. In examining our personal gifts and abilities, it is vital to begin bringing them into their true purpose through connecting fully to Creator and beginning to understand how to use them to express love in its true form.

Each and every one of us within creation is a creative being. We create at every moment. We create because we think a thought and then we take action on it – even if the action is to not do it! We use every trait that we have for creating. Sometimes we don't understand it to be so, for we often apply a very limited and dualistic definition to the act of creativity. For example, we sometimes think only people who paint or sculpt and so on, are creative. But everything is creative! The person who manipulates numbers to make a theory of economics is creative, so is the person who then uses this theory to do their own accounting! These people are being creative with their linear, numerical and sequential traits amongst others; that is, they are making something with them.

The question is: Are they making love? If the economic theory has been created to deceive millions of people, such as the theories running the world's economy have now become, then it is of no true value. Likewise with the painting or the sculpture. If it is created to scare people or to make it seem like something untrue is true, then it has no value.

Because of duality, human beings often form the perception that some traits are "better" than others. For example, there is a common belief right now that it is better to be orderly than to be chaotic. The only thing that is true is that, whether you are chaotic or orderly or some combination thereof, it is only if these traits are used to produce loving outcomes that they have value. The same is true of the concept of give and receive. Giving is not better than receiving and vice versa. It is only when they are used to create love that these traits achieve their true intention and true beauty. And as we said before, simplicity is not better than complexity. It takes both of these traits, used to create love, to encompass all that creation is as an embodiment of love.

We live in a physical world that has moved back and forth from patriarchal forms of governance to matriarchal ones, over and over again throughout its history. Very often, there has been the perception that the opposite of what is currently ruling is the answer to the negative effects espoused throughout its leadership. The end of duality means that human beings will also be able to overcome the perceptions held of the separation between genders, races, sexual preferences and so on and so on – in short, we will be able to cease categorizing everything and applying limiting labels to it and we will be able to simply see the embodiment of love that it is!

It is vital, therefore, to release gender-based (and therefore untruthful) language from the way we reference Creator. Our Creator is not "he" nor is our Creator "she" – our Creator is all that is love. As such our Creator embodies all possible forms love can take. These include forms pre-dating gender as human beings understand it presently. Releasing these forms of dualistic belief-system-based references to our Creator, Source Of All, is a major step in breaking down any dualistic concepts you may hold of it that keep you from experiencing the fullness of its love for you.

Our Creator, the Source Of All, is love and only love. Therefore, everything created from it is love and only love. Remembering that you know this when you are in your soul form, that it is only your physical form that has duality within it and that the new time emerging throughout creation is about bringing all that your soul knows into your body, is a huge concept.

Join your consciousness to that of Creator who made you to love you and to be loved by you and let your every trait, your every thought, your every action be of love. In this way, we and our Creator will create the universe we were meant to live in!

# of love, love and more love

At this time, we need to return to a concept from the beginning of this book – and indeed from the beginning of existence! – and expand upon it for greater understanding.

In the beginning, there was only the energy of love. This love energy decided to create "something" to love and to be loved by. And this love could only create the "something" to love and to be loved by out of what was in existence. Therefore the "something" it created is created out of the pure and absolute energy of love.

Our Creator, Source Of Love, had to "divide" its own energy to create this "something" to love and to be loved by, and this is how the law of duality came into place. The nature of duality has made it appear that there is a separation between ourselves and the love of our Creator and therefore makes it appear that things other than love exist within the physical dimension it applies to.

The energy of duality is present in the cosmic energy field (*aka* the collective consciousness) of all of creation, as is the energy of absolute love.

The new time that is emerging upon the earth is about the cosmic energy field of all of creation becoming unified into absolute love, without duality. This mergence has been happening in actuality in the physical dimension, since December 30, 2006. Prior to that day we as a whole creation were working toward achieving that point in our evolution. We were working toward being able to contain all the love that we are in our physical matter. Duality was one of the laws of existence that enabled the evolution of this container to take place. When we are in our soul form, unencumbered by physical matter's density, we understand this clearly.

Throughout our entire physical evolution the only way we have evolved toward the time of being able to contain all the love that we really are is through loving our Creator and the rest of creation! How perfect! Whenever we have thought of love and acted in love, we have furthered this evolution. Whenever we have thought in duality (non-love) and carried out dualistic (non-loving) actions, we have slowed this evolution.

It is due to all the love we and our Creator have ever done together that we are now able to become what we were truly created to be! Let's celebrate the truth of what we are for it has brought us through duality to this amazing time!

Throughout our evolution to date, the law of duality and the other laws (time, motion, space, gravity, polarity and the dimensions) have governed the physical matter and the energy field of all of creation and of us each, individually. Whenever we have been more connected to the presence of duality energy within the physical dimension than to the true energy of love, we have been buffeted around by the laws themselves. Whenever we have been more connected to the presence of the cosmic and eternal energy of love that is our Creator enacting in love with us, we have been safe.

This has been true throughout our entire physical evolution and, as we enter the age of the end of duality, it continues to be true! Continual connection to love – to being love, to knowing love, to giving love and receiving love – is what we must focus on. And the first step in focusing on it is to know what love is. Knowing what love is is how we know what our Creator truly is and this is how we then know what we truly are! And vice versa.

It is a beautiful and eternal circle of love, fulfilling itself now!

We were created out of love, to love and to be loved. That is the sole (soul) reason we exist. Because we were created out of love, to love and to be loved, our only true need is to love and be loved.

Love is the only true energy of creation. Love meets all needs. It never harms. Love only loves and in so doing, creates more love.

We are love and what created us is love.

Therefore, our sole (soul) purpose is to love and to be loved.

Applying the concept of asking Creator to be with you at every moment of your life and to help you to love and to be loved in everything you do is where you begin to help all of creation move into the time of the end of duality in an active and aware manner. This is how you safely navigate the demise of duality and move into the universe as it was meant to be.

Remembering that the only true need of everything in creation is to love and to be loved and that love meets all needs and never harms is as simple as it needs to be. From there, any amount of complexity can be dealt with!

But without this basic and true definition of love to give our actions and thoughts meaning, the complexity of human living can feel very very overwhelming and hopeless indeed!

We have already outlined many ways of applying this true definition of love to many different scenarios. If you ask Creator to join you in applying it to every situation, whether it is a shopping trip, a holiday, driving to work, making supper, discussing things with a friend, etc, etc; by simply being open to love, you will receive it and it will grow within you answering all need more and more, both for yourself and for others.

the full equation

Understanding that everything we do and are is energy and that this energy is intended to be only love is a big step in our awareness and in our becoming what we have now grown up to become. Being a part of the whole creation that is actively engaged in bringing about the new time of love upon our earth means having our physical matter respond to the energy of love more than it responds to the energy generated by duality and the other laws in ways that limit what we are.

When we ask Creator to help us to be loving and to be loved and for that to be the only energy in our own part of the energy field, we are shifting the cosmic energy field of all of creation into the time of love in the fastest possible way. And it is this simple: ask and receive! In the receiving of this love, you are then giving to the whole! How divine is the circle of love, for it makes every action we do encompassing of us all!

Because we all already make choices from love each and every day, it is easy to make this leap into fuller awareness.

For those who feel that their choices have been much less loving than they should be, simply begin where you are. See where you are enacting love already and expand upon it. Ask Creator to get rid of duality from your energy and matter and to help you proceed into the new time with awareness of what you truly are here for.

The good news is that we all know what to do at some level, for we are all part of a creation that has been heading steadily toward this time ever since it was created. We know what we are. We have just forgotten sometimes when the illusions of duality have blocked us from love.

Even our thoughts of the other laws change when we understand what we are. Does time really affect creation that much, given that we are eternal beings who have been moving in and out of physical form over millions and billions of years? Time affects our physical matter, yes, but it does not affect the vast eternal essence of what we are. When we understand that we are cosmic eternal beings who have evolved through much so that we can become a physical form of love, it helps us to put the dualistic limits of time in perspective, for we have achieved what we have been working toward!

Our cosmic energy field has accumulated the energies of love and non-love throughout our evolution every time we have interacted with one another! Now, as we enter the time of absolute love, we can use this interaction to spread the energy of the new time throughout creation. Again, all one has to do is ask Creator to be with you, sharing this energy through you as a vessel to all the rest of creation. Because it is Creator, whom loves all, this will only be perfect. You do not need to do anything else, other than love the other parts of creation enough to be the vessel of this truly loving energy!

As members of the physical world, where duality exists, we cannot figure out all of the ways in which another part of the creation needs to be healed and brought into the new time. But we can easily facilitate the flow of the love that can. This is where so many of the belief systems and practices of the past, formed in duality, have actually slowed our evolution, for they do not let the true love of our Creator into the physical world to do what only it can do through connection with us! Some of these belief systems make it seem as though we, in isolation, are capable of healing and changing our world for the better and this is not true, for we are only half of the equation! Some of these belief systems have made it seem as though we are helpless in changing the world, as though things are "being done to us" as victims of forces we do not understand! These belief systems do not express the truth that we are active co-creators of our existence.

Working to bring about a place of true healing and true change means drawing on all of the cosmic eternal love that there is, the love that is so magnificent and so powerful that it created all that exists within our amazing, expanding, loving universe! As the "something" created out of love, to love and to be loved, we have been in a state of becoming, not yet fulfilled. Our fulfillment is the new time we are entering. And the only way to get there is to draw closer to the love that created us, that exists eternally and that is co-creating our physical evolution into what we are every step of the way.

This is the magnitude of the love between Creator and Created, for always have we desired to be what we truly are. This desire has guided us through all of the billions of years of duality, as we have maintained focus on exactly what we are doing and where we are going! As stated before, if ever there were times when you as a part of creation strayed out of love and into duality, Creator and every part of creation tried to bring you back to it and the purpose of your very next incarnation was to come back into the balance of love, for yourself, our Creator and the rest of the creation!

We are a magnificent creation, of love. It can be no other way.

the intelligence of love

The only true intelligence in all of existence is love. It is love that has created all and it is love that will heal all. It is love that will endure forever and love that will continue to create. For every question ever asked, love is the answer.

When we work from the intelligence of love first, logic follows because it simply has to. Love is the primary energy of existence, after all. It is the only thing that has meaning. When we look at the world around us, we see how dysfunctional it is and how many things within it have lost meaning. This is duality, creating. Creating from love is what allows things with meaning to exist.

Through the effects of duality, many of our societal structures have lost any sense of direction or purpose they once had. The example of religious institutions is a clear one to use. Once created to teach about our Creator, the religious institute that has become the largest in the world now hoards wealth for the sake of wealth in amounts that would feed all of the hungry of the world! Documents that contain the true word of the love of the Creator are hidden from the world's populace while archaic and meaningless rituals are enacted instead. Fear and superstition are its tools, not love.

Governments and financial bodies operate in much the same way. Although they began as structures designed to meet the needs of the populace, many have long since lost that purpose in any actual way. What the general public sees and what really occurs in the governance of some of the largest and most "powerful" countries in the world are two completely different things.

When we lose sight of the fact that we are one creation, made of love and that our purpose is to love and to be loved, we can see how far the limits and barriers of duality and the other laws can push us. As the time of love unfolds, it will be our co-task to make new structures that are governed by the intelligence of love.

And of course, we already know that the primary need of everything in existence is the very thing it was created for! That is, the primary need of everything in existence is to love and to be loved.

Love meets all needs. And the true need of every living thing is to love and to be loved. Therefore, our true needs get met every time we are loved and every time we are given the opportunity to love.

As we make decisions about how to live in our world and how to co-create the new and loving structures that operate it, the only place to focus is on understanding love and through that understanding, come to co-create structures that enact within it. When we co-create societal structures that address the true need of everyone they interact with, from employees to clients to the greater world and the greater universe, we will have become co-creators of the lives we are truly meant to live.

At all levels of existence, enacting in love is the only solution. Whether you are trying to know what to do in the face of the dualistic behavior of a single person in your life or trying to know what to do in the face of the dualistic governing bodies of our world, it all begins with true connection to Creator who made us all to love us and to be loved by us. It all begins with understanding the true definition of love and applying it to whatever situation is in front of us. Through understanding love, we can move past being affected by the harmful behavior of others and into a state of getting our true needs met while allowing others to do the same. This is the only true solution there is for it is the only solution that does not create a new problem even as it tries to solve an old one.

we, in love

Looking past the dualistic behavior of others means recognizing that they also are made out of the love of our Creator but that the energy of duality has made them forget this. You can help change this. Offering to be a vessel of our Creator's love is all that you need to do. Our Creator can flow through you, healing you and them of all duality and bringing you both more into the new time. You don't have to know all of the things that have contributed to their behavior because that would be trying to understand untruth and, as we said before, this is not where our energy and our intelligence needs to be used. Creator knows what they need, in minute detail! All it needs is an open vessel to love through in order to provide what they need. If they are so blocked up by duality that they can create bombs, or plan economic upheavals or attempt to launch pandemics, they obviously are not able to be a clear vessel for love to flow into!

The true enactment of love, on your part, is to be a "doorway" through which the massive amount of cosmic Creator love these people need can enter and bring about an end to their duality! Simply by offering to do this, you are elevating yourself into becoming more and more of a being of unified love, for you have met the true need of that person, yourself and our Creator!

And because Creator's love only encompasses all, it heals you as it flows.

Remember that this was created to be an interactive relationship! As you need to love and to be loved, so does what created you! The only desire of our Creator is to love and to be loved. Therefore, when we take steps to ensure this happens we are making love occur on a cosmic and infinite scale! Connecting to our Creator and moving into a loving relationship with it that allows it to give you the gifts of love it desires to give you, and asking it to flow through you to do the same thing for all of the rest of creation, is love in action, love eternal, love unfolding to be what it was meant to be!

And this is the truth of love, of course. When we open ourselves to any part of it, it only grows! Focusing on your personal co-creative relationship with Creator and asking it to free you of all the duality you have accumulated in your "portion" of the cosmic energy field means there is that much less duality energy in the whole cosmic energy field! This means more of creation is freed of duality too and can move closer to loving and being loved by Creator! Give and receive! Perfect, easy and divine!

Because you are operating from the true intelligence of love, you can now understand that the dualistic things said about our Creator throughout our evolution are not truth. You can overcome them and come into understanding that our living, loving and miraculous Creator wants only to love and to be loved. You can share and enjoy the many gifts of love with Creator and, in so doing, discover and co-create more of them!

All that you are, when used for love, is love in an embodiment! Because you embody it for the purposes of love, it is a facet of Creator, also. Your particular sense of humour, the way you like to dress, the way you express yourself, and so on and so on... all of these, when used for love, are the gifts of love that you contain! So being who you are with who made you is exactly what you need to be. There is no "procedure" or "protocol" to this. In fact, many of the procedures and protocols of the past actually have created a greater sense of separation! All there needs to be is a desire to interact. How it begins is by asking and knowing that it is occurring. How much duality you have will directly affect how quickly and easily you experience the loving results but stick with it and you will see them. Throughout our entire evolution, love has never given up on you so don't give up on it!

When we understand that we are choosing to be love because love is what we are and are made of, choosing to interact with our Creator is a "no-brainer". It is the only thing that makes any sense because love is the only intelligent sense there is. It is the only thing that is real, true, eternal and limitless. It is we.

love. now is the time.

Love is easy. Love is the easiest thing there is to do. Again, it is duality that has caused us to carry beliefs that say otherwise. We are love and love is our true state. If you are finding it hard to love, you are carrying a lot of duality in your "portion" of the cosmic energy field. Because energy is what we are made of, the dualistic energy you carry is affecting your thoughts and the function of your body. Again, the only answer is to ask Creator, Source Of All Love, to clear the duality out of your energy field so that you can feel the truth of what you are.

Because duality energy affects our thoughts and our physical matter, a major part of being free of it is to make sure the needs of our bodies and minds are met in the physical dimension. Because you are loved, an addendum about the nutrition you need is attached to this book. Our

Creator, who loves you and wants to co-create with you, is urging you to get the nutrition you need to feed your physical matter so it is not generating a primal energy of lack into your energy field. If affording the nutrition is not a possibility at this time, focus on greater and greater connection and to clearing out more and more duality energy and the means to get what you need will come to you.

The time of love is unfolding. We will soon be a part of a world where need will no longer exist. How we get there is by focusing the power of the energy that we are (love) with the power of what created us (love) to bring it about.

It is all so simple. But then so is love! The definition of love that we have given here is very very simple. Applying it and re-applying it to complex issues is how we solve them.

It is all so simple and so clear because love is never changing! And even as it never changes, so too does it ever change! That is love. It does it all as long as it is love!

Connecting to our Creator, the Source Of Love That Made All, to bring about the time of love for all in creation is also easy. All you need to do is ask. Until you break down all barriers that keep this love out, it is necessary to ask and ask and ask. This is your role in being a co-creator. In time, you will not have to ask. You and Creator will be fully connected, enacting in love and unity and helping this to come to fulfillment for all of creation!

And of course, we already know that the primary need of everything in existence is the very thing it was created for! That is, the primary need of everything in existence is to love and to be loved.

Love meets all needs. And the true need of every living thing is to love and to be loved. Therefore, our true needs get met every time we are loved and every time we are given the opportunity to love.

Ask Creator to remove all duality (non-love) energy from you and from your energy field and replace it with the true energy of love that you and Creator are. Ask Creator to join with you and do the same thing for all of creation. Ask Creator to use you as a vessel of its love and bring the energy of love to all that you are surrounded with. In any way you can think of and in any way that comes to you as a message from Creator, ask Creator to show you love and give you love and give love back to it. Ask Creator what else you can do to help the new time come about, the time when love will be the only energy governing creation and all duality will be gone.

Love everyone and everything, including yourself and Creator in this way. We are entering the age of miracles. We are a miracle of love and have been so since the moment of our creation. Let us now live as what we were created to be. It is the time of love.

addendum

Nutrition for the Unified (Non-Dualistic) Brain
(Abridged from the Time of love Manual*)*

Because the Time of Love is about healing and unifying your whole being: body, mind, heart and soul, nutrition is *vital*.

The Time of Love is about creating the unified (non-dualistic) brain capable only of thoughts of love and of truth, and Omega 3 oil is the nutrient needed most to accomplish this quickly.

We are thought made manifest as matter and action! A healed, fully nourished brain can only hold healthy, positive and true thoughts leading to *loving* actions, while an unhealed and undernourished brain will struggle to retain such thinking or may even be unable to.

We are thought made manifest as matter and action! A unified brain that is incapable of thoughts of duality, will only think thoughts of love, for that is our true state. Therefore love is what we will be able to create in all of its fullness, without duality.

For you to fully experience the results of this material as rapidly as possible, you must commit to the physical and nutritional healing of your body and brain matter.

An unhealed and underfed brain can interfere with your ability to communicate with Creator as you begin to unify your whole being, to understand the truth of what love is and other true concepts, to remember past lives to access the love (and not the trauma) there, to become free of fear and other untruths, etc.

Many people have brain injuries. These range from slight to severe. Brain injuries can be caused by such things as bumps on the head, malnutrition, the process of birth, ingestion of brain-damaging substances, etc.

It should be noted that the single largest factor in brain injury today is malnutrition.

People simply are not feeding their brain the types of nutritional components it needs to be fully functional and healed to cope with modern day life, let alone proceed with Creator into the Time of Love and the end of duality.

What's more, many common modern day foods affect brain function negatively. One of the non-foods commonly eaten that damages brain cells is artificial fats. This includes all hydrogenated and partially hydrogenated oils such as margarine and processed oils.

All brain healing protocols must include removal of these non-foods from the diet. Margarine must be replaced with butter or other natural fats (nerve endings are made out of components contained in butter in great concentration). Processed oils that can survive for long periods of time in cupboards are already severely altered. They must be replaced by unrefined olive oil, grapeseed oil, coconut oil and other unrefined oils.

Processed cheese products such as cheese spread and slices should be absolutely avoided. Replace them with traditionally prepared hard and soft cheeses.

Stress is another factor that is contributing to brain malnutrition. The human brain is intended to be comprised of a large percentage of omega-3 fat! All hormones contain omega-3 as a base. Dopamine (the feel good hormone), serotonin (for mood balance) and melatonin (deep restful sleep) all contain large amounts of omega-3. Insulin, estrogen, progesterone, testosterone, etc. all have omega-3 as a base. Adrenal hormones that are used in times of stress also have omega-3 as a base.

At the present time, we are using our stress hormones and adrenal system far far more than we ever have before and far more than it is designed to be used. Stress is depleting the entire endocrine system and brain system of its omega-3 content at very rapid rates. The adrenal glands are as crucial to life as the heart and liver and brain; therefore our bodies are often having to make difficult choices over how to share its limited resources if we are omega-3 deficient and stressed .

The good news is that our miraculous bodies can do it all when given enough to work with!

Never before has the human race lived with the amount of stress we live with! Never before have we been able to injure ourselves so severely at the speeds we can attain or so easily with the activities we do. Never before have we ingested substances – legal and illegal – capable of damaging our brains *instantly.* And some of these substances we are consuming as food! (For example: artificial sweeteners, colorings and flavorings.)

With all these factors considered it is no wonder we have a great need for omega-3 even before the work to create the unified brain and 12-strand DNA begins. Many "diseases" we accept as a natural part of life are actually omega-3 deficiency states. Things like PMS and menopause, erectile dysfunction and lack of libido, learning and behavioral problems, road rage and forgetfulness are all helped immensely by adequate consumption of omega-3.

The body's natural stress response was only ever intended to be used occasionally. We now use it on a daily basis. The more stress we have and the more intellectual challenges we face, the more omega-3 we will use up.

A suitable analogy to use here is: The faster and farther you drive the car, the more fuel you need.

And now we are driving the car into a new world, one of absolute love! Our Creator Who Is Only Love is at the wheel!

The truth is that, as magnificently complex and amazing it is, the physical body is only comprised of seven things: proteins; carbohydrates; fats (of which omega-3 should be the most in abundance); a handful of vitamins; 73 minerals; water and the energy of the Source Of Our Creation, Who Is Only Love!

We are inviting Creator, Source Of All Love, in to heal us as never before – let's give it the materials it needs to do this rapidly! And one of the main materials we need is omega-3.

feed your brain

At the present time Creator recommends a liquid omega-3 oil with at least 750mg EPA and 500mg DHA per teaspoon. This is the ratio that occurs in nature. Look for products that have been unaltered in the "lab" except perhaps to concentrate them. There are some exceptional brands of fish oil around that have been molecularly distilled to remove toxins and are also very good tasting. If you are a vegetarian, coconut oil is an excellent source of omega-3 and is very concentrated as well. A tablespoon of fish oil or a tablespoon and a half of coconut oil daily meets the needs of most people. Or you can choose products like hemp oil or flax oil that, again, have been unaltered in a lab. These require tablespoons versus teaspoons but mix into shakes and smoothies well. In other parts of the world, rich sources of omega-3 exist and can be used in place of what is articulated here. Those with brain injuries naturally will require more.

Please note that the body can make omega-6 and 9 out of omega-3, but cannot break down naturally occurring 6 and 9 into 3 if it needs it. Therefore purchasing a lab-created omega 3-6-9 product is unnecessary and money is best spent on a concentrated but otherwise unaltered natural omega-3 product.

At present we are not able to eat enough omega-3-containing foods to meet the needs of our stressful and intellectual lives, let alone meet the needs of our brains as we move forward into the new consciousness of the Time of Love!

We recommend starting with a minimum of 3 teaspoons or the equivalent a day based on the above EPA/DHA ratio. Keep in mind that you can take less, but your healing time will increase exponentially. In that case it is a good idea to also add a soluble fiber like ground brown flaxseed or hemp. This is very good for the liver and adds a helping of omega-3 if enough is eaten. *(See chart, page 135).*

People with emotional and/or physical trauma from their current life or with excessive past life sorrow or addictions or brain injuries etc. also require higher intake of omega-3. Paying attention to your body's cues that indicate it wants more oil is the best way to determine your personal dosage. Cravings for the oil are a good sign! Cravings for junk foods are also an indicator that more omega-3 is needed. These cravings will cease as the true requirements of your body are met with consistency.

Consistency with meeting your needs for omega-3 and the other nutrients listed in this addendum is hugely significant, not only on a physical level, but also on a energy field level. If you are inconsistent with the nutrition, you are allowing the energy of not having enough of what you truly need to be present in your energy field. This kind of subconscious energy can prevent you from manifesting what you need in your life and in your coming into the Time of Love as quickly as you could. You must not miss a day of taking the nutrition if at all possible.

If you have liver problems or emotional issues of non-deservance, etc., it is possible that you will find it difficult to take the oil. If this is the case, simply start with a very small amount and work your way up. Persevere. There is always a solution, even if you must begin with rubbing coconut oil on your body instead of ingesting it. You are a cosmic eternal being of love and you have the ability to overcome these issues. Work with constant communication with Creator to break down these dualistic barriers.

Creator will work on removing emotional issues that stand between you and accepting true healing first. You are more than able to be an active co-creator in your true healing now that you have the information you need!

The chart below offers some alternative ratios to straight fish oil so that you can enjoy some variety as you take your omega-3.

Equivalent Measures for Omega 3 (approximate)
1 teaspoon fish oil with 750mg EPA/500mg DHA =
    1 1/4 tablespoons flax oil
    2 1/2 tablespoons ground brown flax
    4-10 wild salmon capsules *(check strength)*
    6-14 flax oil capsules *(check strength)*
    2 tablespoons hemp seeds
    1 tablespoon hemp oil
    1 1/2 teaspoons unrefined coconut oil *(can be used for cooking or as a body lotion)*

You can see that the fish oils are very, very efficient. For short trips take it with you and keep it in an ice bucket or cooler. For longer trips, hemp seed is a good travelling companion to help keep dosages up. So is coconut oil because it does not require refrigeration and is also very efficient to take.

Several companies now have concentrated capsules available. Some capsules unfortunately contain substances that are very hard to break down by the body and that have a non-food component to them so be cautious when purchasing, but these can also be a part of your nutritional routine when travelling.

hydration

Proper hydration increases our cellular energy which contributes to greater energy over all! It also helps us get rid of toxins. The reason for this is simple: the human body is about 70% water. Therefore, water is the main medium in which cellular activity occurs. If there is not enough water, cellular movement is sluggish and this contributes to sluggishness and lack of energy as symptoms we experience. It also contributes to toxic matter staying within our tissues.

Hydration is a two part equation that involves both consumption and utilization. Consumption involves taking in adequate hydrating fluids. These include water and natural, non-caffeinated beverages.

Utilization involves taking in adequate amounts of electrolytes.

The easiest and most natural way to do this is through the consumption of true salt.

What is true salt?

True salt is salt that has not been refined!

In other words: You need to consume unrefined natural sea salt or inland salt from an old sea bed, and avoid refined salt completely.

When salt (or any other food) is refined, molecules displace other molecules. This results in an alteration to the product itself. Refined salt is almost devoid of electrolyte balancing minerals. It is difficult or impossible for the kidneys to use white, bleached salt to balance fluids throughout the body.

All life on this planet began in salt water. A trace amount of complete salt is required by our bodies to get fluids into tissue properly and to get fluids to travel "uphill" against gravity to properly hydrate our brain and our spinal cord. An astonishing number of people have low amounts of cerebro-spinal fluid. This important brain-nourishing solution is comprised of omega-3 and water *and* it takes electrolytes to get it to the brain and keep it there!

Stress plays a large role in depleting our electrolytes because our adrenal glands and renal glands (kidneys) play an important role in electrolyte balance. Stress uses up electrolytes.

A lot of people also do not experience thirst. This is partly because electrolytes play an important role in thirst response.

As we enter the Time of Love, we are seeing a large number of "diseases" that are actually caused by lack of proper hydration. High blood pressure and thick blood are two illnesses that are greatly helped by the consumption of small amounts of true salt and adequate water! Joint degeneration and muscle pain and tightness is also greatly helped by consuming true salt and water as well as omega-3. And, fluid retention problems go away with the proper consumption of true salt to balance the body's ability to use fluids and to give the kidneys and adrenal glands what they need to function properly.

It only takes a pinch a day! We recommend making certain that you have a small amount ($1/16$ - $1/8^{th}$ of a teaspoon or so) per day of true salt.

If you don't eat salt – *you need to, but choose the right one!*

In the energy field, lack of "flow" in one's life can be one of the symptoms of dehydration and improper electrolyte balance. We want ease in moving forward into the Time of Love. A few grains of true salt can help this negative energy to dissipate from your life.

Remember that the human body in a healthy state is capable of tolerating small quantities of things that are not "good" for us. For example, a cup or two of coffee in a well-hydrated body is a wonderful treat for those who love the flavor and can be enjoyed without guilt. Likewise a drink or two of alcohol.

For those who choose to have coffee etc., we have included words for healing and raising the vibration of the "unhealthy" things we consume. It follows at the end of this section. Adding your words and intent to the process only amplifies it and speeds the process up. It involves you as active co-creator of love, which is what you were created to be.

Alcohol consumption beyond one or two drinks requires extra oils due to its effects on brain matter. If you are taking a lot of oil as it is you may wish to avoid alcohol or severely restrict it. Using the love energy of Creator to do healing on the alcohol will help and should always be done. The general rule of thumb (and a great way to avoid a hangover) is to take enough oil to get 2400mg EPA/1500mg DHA and a large glass of water with a pinch of unrefined sea salt before imbibing. Repeat the procedure when you are done if you have had more than 3 drinks. Do this again in the morning if you are still tired or feel hungover. This prevents loss of brain cells and therefore prevents setbacks.

other nutrition

A healthy body has healthy cravings!

You are working with Creator and as you heal you will naturally find yourself craving healthy substances.

If you are deficient in basic nutrition, try a green drink or juicing as opposed to a multivitamin, or make a concerted effort to eat many more vegetables and fruit. We are designed to eat whole foods and it is difficult to get a balance of vitamins and minerals out of isolated "lab-made" components. The simple addition of nuts and seeds (raw always) and sprouts will contribute far more minerals and vitamins (and the accompanying enzymes to utilize them) than a pill! There is far more usable calcium in greens than in a supplement.

Zinc is one of the minerals most present in the human brain (it is involved in synapses) and is one of the minerals most used when the body is healing. Many people who are proceeding into the Time of Love and the brain evolution this entails are discovering they have high needs for zinc.

Zinc is used in more than 200 enzymes in the body. It is best to simply include a green drink or raw pumpkin seeds and so on in the daily diet right from the outset, and avoid deficiency problems later. Again, zinc made in a lab can be insufficient but can be added if you are very deficient. Look for whole food sources (raw pumpkin seeds, oysters, etc.) or homeopathic zinc if possible. Signs that you are zinc deficient can include low energy, lack of mental clarity, bladder issues, erectile dysfunction, and slow healing. If in doubt, try adding zinc and seeing how you feel! Be open to receiving loving messages from Creator about what else you need. Calcium and magnesium are two important minerals to maintain a balance of as well.

If your body weight is out of balance, that too will shift as you heal.

love for healing foods, etc.

This is very useful during healing time to ensure that you are getting the full benefit of the goods you are consuming, wearing, etc. Once your unified energy reaches a certain point it will no longer be necessary to do this because the goods will be healed just by the unified touch of yourself and Creator. Some people like to continue to say this anyway because it is very loving. And of course, change the words to suit yourself.

> CREATOR WHOM IS ONLY LOVE
> Please heal this _____
> (food, beverage, supplement, meal, etc.)
> So that it is perfect for my consumption
> In every way. Thank you.

more about your beautiful brain as it becomes non-dualistic

It is estimated that the average human being uses 26% or less of their "grey matter". When you think about all the amazing things we do on just that small percent, think of what we could accomplish with more! What is the rest there for? And what does it contain?

It contains your eternal consciousness – who you truly are and have been across all of your evolution and everything you know!

Developing new thinking to expand beyond our current five physical senses means that the brain must be healed beyond just the senses required to live on the purely physical dimensions. Living within the limits of our five physical senses means maintaining an unawareness of all that we truly are!

Tapping into and easily accessing the truth gained in our evolution and the all-encompassing love of our souls and Creator requires a fully healed and unified brain.

Being completely free of fear, ego, untruth and all other products of duality that are not love requires a fully healed and unified brain.

Understanding new concepts and putting together whole concepts requires a fully healed and functioning brain. A fully unified brain leads to limitless creativity and ability.

Accessing concepts that are new and those that are not new but were known at the dawn of your creation and that are in your consciousness requires brain feeding and unification.

Becoming whole-brained (all lobes and abilities fully activated and functioning) and staying that way requires brain food. To merge body, mind, heart and soul with Creator and become your true non-dualistic being requires a fully healed brain as it is the "circuit board" for your whole being.

Learning new skills necessary for your purpose in bringing about the Time of Love and re-awakening old ones requires a fully healed brain. Our purpose has evolved through time with us and will continue to evolve. A fully healed brain finds it easy to learn and is unaffected by stress.

The healing of emotional issues and physical issues and gaining new understandings of what it means to be our true whole being of love requires a fully healed brain.

Developing the non-dualistic neural pathways that enable us to access Creator and our souls fully for the Time of Love requires brain feeding. This is the new consciousness that all in creation will be evolving in from now on!

further information and resources for the time of love

This addendum is an excerpt from the Nutrition chapter in *The Time of Love Manual*, which is available as a free download from our website, **www.thetimeoflove.com.** *The Time of Love Manual* and other loving books and materials are available to help you become an active co-creator of the Time of Love. The manual is also available as a printed book from the Time of Love website and Amazon.com.

www.thetimeoflove.com

Like love, our website is growing and wants to encompass more and more co-creation; please visit our website to read Christine's blog and participate in our interactive online community. Many more publications, video and audio productions will be added throughout 2010 and onward!

the love collection

The next book in *The Love Collection* is *Why Everything Happens (Or the Truth of Everything in Existence)*. If you would like to stay connected with *The Love Collection* series, sign up for the newsletter on our website, www.thetimeoflove.com.

www.ingramcontent.com/pod-product-compliance
Lightning Source LLC
Chambersburg PA
CBHW070809100426
42742CB00012B/2309